COLLEGE LIBRARY

Forgotten Victims is published by Planet Publishing

Copyright © 1994 Design and artwork: Planet Publishing Ltd.
Copyright © 1994 Text: Paula Casey.

The right of Paula Casey to be identified as the author of this work has been asserted in accordance with the English Copyright Designs and Patents Act 1988, Sections 77 and 78.

Original paintings by Gerard Duxel

All rights reserved. No part of this publication may be reproduced, stored in a retrieval system or transmitted in any form or by any means, electronic, electrostatic, magnetic tape, mechanical, photocopying, recording or otherwise, without permission in writing from the publishers.

First Edition 1994

A CIP catalogue record for this book is available from the British Library.

Planet Publishing Ltd. UK Address: 20 Berkeley Street, London W1X5AE.

BRITANNIA ROYAL NAVAL COLLEGE LIBRARY

BOOK No. 43924

956.7 : 342.7

CONTENTS

Introduction	5
Arrest and Detention	9
The Human Tragedy	23
Efforts to Release the Prisoners	41
Legal Background	59
Conclusions	72
Footnotes	74

INTRODUCTION

On 2 August 1990, Kuwait, a small oil-rich country situated at the head of the Arabian Gulf, was invaded by its powerful, belligerent neighbour, Iraq. The brutal occupation which ensued, and the events which finally ended in the dramatic liberation of Kuwait on 26 February 1991, have been well-documented elsewhere. It is not the purpose of this book to cover that ground again, except in so far as it forms the background to a humanitarian issue that still festers three years after liberation: i.e. the fate of hundreds of Kuwaiti citizens and third-country nationals detained by the Iraqis during the occupation.

Kuwait was, of course, extremely pleased that the ruthless Iraqi occupying force was ousted from its territory, however nothing could have adequately prepared its citizens for the enormous task of rebuilding their ravaged nation. Structurally, major strides were made in a very short space of time. Raging oil-fires that belched black smoke across the oil-strewn desert were miraculously quenched in less than 10 months, and a vast quantity of live ordnance including land mines, hidden by the shifting sands, was rendered harmless. Many of the public buildings maliciously destroyed or looted by the Iraqis in order to eradicate any traces of Kuwaiti culture and national identity were rapidly rebuilt. Kuwait's inhabitants also set about the difficult task of cleaning away the debris and filth left behind in their public institutions, private and commercial premises. Shops were opened and looted goods replaced.

Little now remains to remind the visitor to Kuwait of the physical destruction wrought by the Iraqis. However, there are deep wounds in the psyche of the Kuwaiti nation which will take much longer to mend. The savage treatment meted out to the local population has left an indelible legacy. The fact that Iraq, three years after the war has officially ended, still refuses to release, or at the very least account for, around 600 Kuwaiti citizens[1] prolongs the intolerable suffering and the prospect of healing for much of the Kuwaiti population. Kuwaiti society, which is based on an extended family structure, is intensely close-knit. In a population of approximately 850,000 Kuwaiti nationals anxiety over the fate of almost 600 of their people affects almost every member of that society.

The western world, on the other hand, appears to be somewhat immune to this tragedy. Imagine the uproar if the equivalent percentage of westerners, say for example, 200,000 Americans or 50,000 British people were detained by a ruthless tyrant who refused to provide any information concerning their whereabouts or even acknowledge their existence? The fact that there are many other on-going tragedies in the world today does not lessen the anger, grief and despair experienced by the relatives of those Kuwaitis whose fate, following the end of the war, remains a mystery[2]. Nor does it help that this is a problem which frequently follows war. Over twenty years after its withdrawal from Vietnam, the United States of America is still searching for its soldiers missing in action (MIAs) in that country. A major difference between the Kuwait and Vietnamese situations is that Vietnam is now opening its doors to the outside world and, in its eagerness to gain international credibility, it is giving every facility to the USA to search for and ascertain the fate of missing persons. Nevertheless, the specialized American team orchestrating the search is experiencing considerable difficulty in carrying out its task. It does not take a great leap of imagination therefore to appreciate the problems associated with locating missing persons under a paranoid Iraqi regime which must have one of the worst records of human rights violations in recent years.

This book sets out to examine the issues associated with locating Kuwait's missing persons. The pattern of arrests and detentions during the occupation as well as the treatment of persons so detained are briefly described. An attempt is also made to put a human face on the statistics by describing the harrowing experiences of a number of relatives whose loved ones are still missing. Kuwait's efforts to secure the release of missing persons are thoroughly examined, as are the efforts of

Introduction

international bodies. The issues surrounding the arrest, detention, release and repatriation of civilian and military personnel are also placed in the context of international humanitarian law, the body of law which seeks to protect the victims of armed conflict. Finally, conclusions are drawn and recommendations are made with a view towards arriving at a resolution of this difficult humanitarian problem.

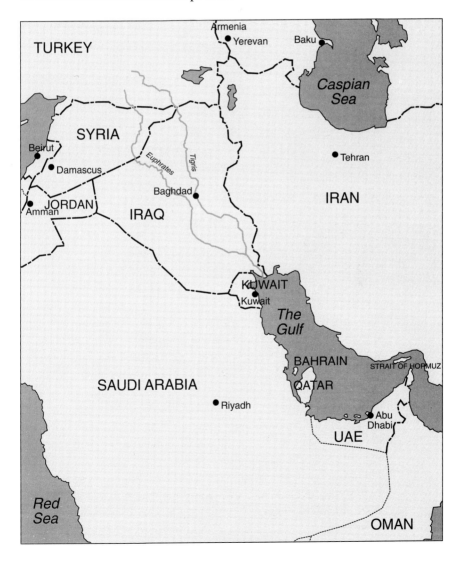

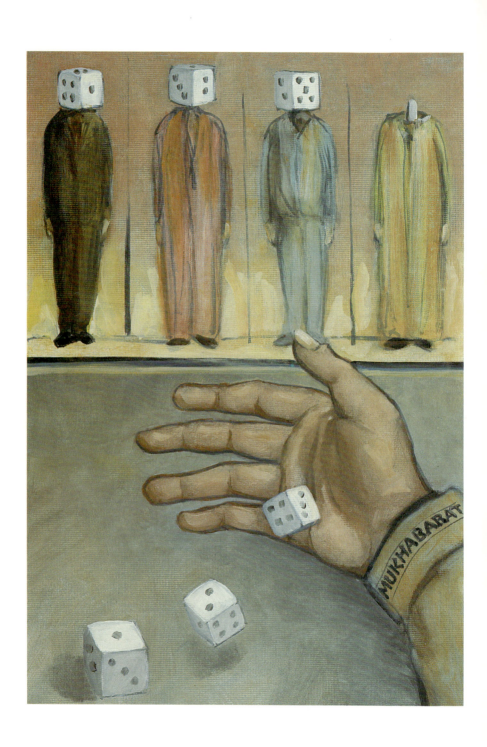

ARREST AND DETENTION

It is hoped that a brief factual description of the situation which pertained in Kuwait during the occupation, and some analysis of the reasons for the many arrests and detentions of Kuwaiti and third country nationals will help the reader to understand the plight of persons presently imprisoned in Iraq.

Prisoners of war

A considerable number of people were killed and many more were taken prisoner during the fighting which accompanied the invasion, and in its immediate aftermath. Those imprisoned included members of the armed forces who were actively resisting the numerically-superior Iraqi army as well as important figures in the Kuwaiti administration. Military personnel captured during this early period, for the most part, were granted prisoner of war status and sent to camps in Iraq. Most of this group was not subjected to torture[1], and even though camp conditions were harsh, they were better than those experienced by the majority of civilian internees. Over 600 officers (military and police)[2] were detained at Ba'qooba, 55km from Baghdad, having spent periods of time at al-Rashid and a camp at al-Mosul. Others were detained at camps in al-Ramadi, and Tikrit. Although visits to these camps by the International Committee of the Red Cross (ICRC) were not permitted by the Iraqi authorities, it did prove possible for some prominent Kuwaitis to arrange for families to visit their detained relatives in Iraq from the beginning of October 1990. An office was opened in Kuwait to register families who wished to visit Iraq for this purpose. These visits ensured that the prisoners received much-needed supplies, and the news from home helped to reassure them concerning the welfare of their families. The opportunity to use the Iraqi telephone system to communicate with relatives outside of Kuwait was an added attraction for Kuwaitis wishing to make the difficult journey north.

Brutality of the Iraqi occupation

A second broad group of persons was arrested as the occupation continued and it became obvious that the inhabitants of Kuwait[3] were not enamoured with the all-embracing Iraqi presence, and were not prepared to succumb to the tyranny of the occupying forces, nor to concur in the erasure of the Kuwaiti national identity. August and September 1990 were particularly productive for the *Mukhabarat*, the notorious Iraqi secret police, who attempted to spread their unique brand of terror across the borders into Kuwait through systematic house searches and random checkpoint controls. Some of this second group were members of military and police forces (including reservists and retired members) who had evaded detection in the initial sweep of arrests. If readily identifiable as military personnel, they were usually detained as prisoners of war. Others were civilians who held important posts in the Kuwaiti administration, or civilians who for some reason or another fell foul of the Iraqis. To understand the reasons, spurious or otherwise, for these numerous arrests, detentions and deportations, it is necessary to briefly describe life in Kuwait under Iraqi occupation.

The well-ordered and secure life of Kuwait's citizens had been turned upside down by the invasion. Once the initial fighting had subsided, a general air of insecurity and fear was all-pervasive as 'normal' life came to a stand-still. Thousands of Kuwaiti and third-country nationals had attempted to flee the country. Schools and other institutions were closed and the impressive Kuwaiti health service was devastated by the flight of intimidated expatriate workers as well as the eviction of patients, commandeering of hospital beds, and the pillaging of essential medical equipment by Iraqi forces. Money was scarce, banks had closed down and most private companies had folded since the commercial sector had been ravaged by widespread looting. Workers, including civil servants who had refused to turn up for work except in essential services such as water and electricity, were without salaries. Food was a problem; cooperative supermarkets[4], often manned by volunteers, remained open, but with vastly depleted stocks.

Arrest and Detention

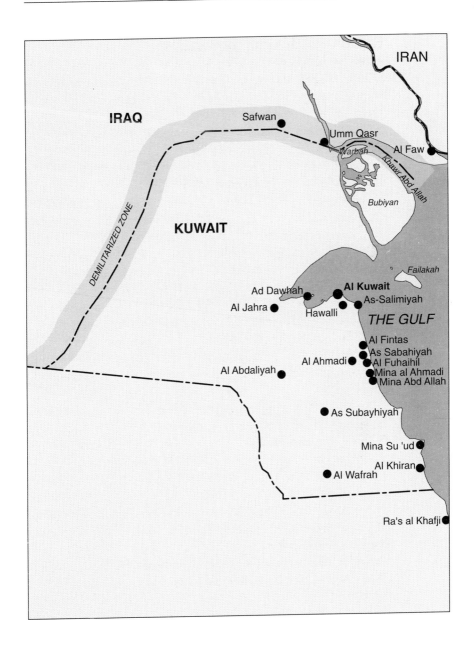

A wide range of harmless acts of defiance against the occupying force, such as possession of a portrait of the Emir, or the Kuwaiti national flag, or refusal to hang a picture of Saddam Hussein in place of that of the Emir, frequently met with a savage response from the Iraqi forces: arrest, detention, and sometimes even summary execution. Prayer-leaders who petitioned God for the liberation of Kuwait during the regular Friday prayers were also arrested. Harassment during house searches, and at the many checkpoints on the main thoroughfares and secondary streets throughout the country, was commonplace. Women were often subjected to lewd and obscene insults at checkpoints and an angry reaction on the part of their menfolk was sufficient reason for arrest. Several arbitrary executions also took place at checkpoints[5].

Iraq promulgated numerous penal orders during September and October 1990, many of which were aimed at the Iraqization of Kuwait[6]. In particular Kuwaiti citizens were obliged, as of 1 October 1990, to exchange their Kuwaiti identity papers for Iraqi identity cards and to change their car licence plates for Iraqi ones identifying Kuwait as an Iraqi province. Other decrees ordered Kuwaitis to surrender their weapons or face execution if found in possession of guns. The Iraqis also threatened to demolish houses from which shots were fired, together with surrounding properties in a radius of 360 degrees[7].

The compulsory replacement of identity cards and vehicle registration was largely unsuccessful because the vast majority of Kuwaitis refused to comply with the Iraqi demands since this would have effectively signalled a change in nationality. This refusal meant that it eventually became extremely difficult to drive, obtain petrol, or receive the meagre hospital treatment that was still available. The necessary ration cards for basic foods such as milk, sugar, rice, flour and cooking oil were also unobtainable without Iraqi identity documents. However, Kuwaitis evaded arrest by pleading that there were long queues at the Traffic Departments until the final deadline was adopted on 22 January 1991. After the outbreak of the air-war, it was no longer possible to drive a Kuwaiti registered car without risking confiscation and/or arrest. Indeed, drivers of the more coveted models were particularly prone to being arrested and having their cars confiscated. In addition, if an individual was driving the car of a family member and therefore his ID did not match the car documents, he or she would frequently be detained and the car confiscated never to be seen again.

A central committee of prominent Kuwaitis tried to restore some kind of order and structure to Kuwaiti society, and to channel aid in the form of medicines, food and money to needy people in Kuwait. Each district had also formed a committee, composed of local leaders and cooperative managers, which sought to take charge of these matters in their own area. Many committee members were simply involved in organizing medicine and health-care for the local inhabitants and delivering food supplies to house bound friends, neighbours, and relatives including old-people and women, whose menfolk were either out of the country at the time of the invasion, or had already been killed or arrested by the Iraqis. Institutions such as hospitals and homes for the mentally handicapped also needed to be supplied with food.

Money[8] was smuggled into the country from the Kuwaiti Government-in-exile, based in Saudi Arabia, and distributed amongst needy inhabitants, including those in hiding from the Iraqis. Some of those involved in the distribution of food and money were arrested by the Iraqis and accused of 'economic sabotage'. In addition, the constant flow of young people engaged in this work made the *Mukhabarat* and their informers extremely suspicious that activities other than humanitarian relief were being carried out. The Iraqi net was thrown extremely wide drawing in those who were acting entirely peacefully as well as those actively engaged in supporting military resistance. For example, a number of Kuwaitis were arrested crossing the border from Saudi Arabia to Kuwait: some were bringing money for humanitarian purposes; others were carrying money and weapons; others simply wished to ensure that close relatives were safe.

A portion of the food and money distributed by Kuwaitis was given to the approximately 2,000 westerners who had avoided being transported to Iraq along with other third-State nationals, many of whom were being held in appaling conditions at military sites around Iraq[9]. These people remained in hiding in Kuwait, moving from one location to another to avoid detection, often secreting themselves in air-conditioning ducts as Iraqi soldiers ransacked their 'safe' houses. All were dependent on friends and neighbours to provide them with food and hiding places. Although Iraq had already warned Kuwaitis that they risked the severest punishment if they sheltered, or rendered assistance to foreigners[10], many Kuwaitis risked their freedom and their lives to help those nationalities such as American and British who were wanted by the Iraqis. Other foreign nationals, including New Zealanders, Australian and Irish, were allowed relative freedom of movement and were also able to support their friends. Most westerners were permitted to leave Kuwait at the beginning of December, although a few remained until liberation.

Resistance to the Iraqi occupation took many forms. Sometimes, it involved information-gathering and transmittal through the satellite communications system which had been rescued from the Ministry of Communications. By the end of the first week of the invasion, daily communications had been re-established with the Kuwaiti Government in Saudi Arabia, and with the Kuwaiti Embassy in Washington DC. Much information on conditions in occupied Kuwait was passed through these networks. Resistance members were even in direct communication with American television networks in an attempt to highlight the plight of those remaining in Kuwait. Kuwait Oil Company personnel used another satellite system to direct allied air strikes on Iraqi positions and the pumping manifolds which were pouring oil into the Gulf. Other resistance members forged driving licences, car registration books, identity cards etc. for their compatriots. Attempts were also made by resistance groups to rescue vital data from government buildings. Some people published and distributed resistance newsletters or sprayed anti-Iraqi graffiti on walls. A favourite slogan was: "Allah, Al-Watan, Al-Amir! (God, The Nation, The Amir). Others attacked the large outdoor portraits of Saddam Hussein which had appeared all over Kuwait.

Not all resistance members were involved in non-violent activity. Several members of the ruling Al-Sabah family had remained in or returned to Kuwait to fight. They joined up with resistance groups included high-ranking personnel from the National Guard, the Air Force, and the police, who had managed to evade arrest, as well as civilians, both men and women, from every walk of life. Hit-and run attacks on Iraqi positions and road-blocks were organized, especially in the period from August to November before arrests and executions made it extremely difficult for armed resistance to continue.

Reprisals by the Iraqis for all kinds of resistance activities were swift and without mercy and, as promised, collective penalties were often directed against those who had no direct part in the resistance. Others arrested were merely suspected of such involvement, perhaps on the slimmest of evidence. Sometimes the entire family of the suspect, father, mother and even young siblings, was detained. Thirty-seven members of one particular extended family were either killed or arrested; two are amongst the persons still missing. Doctors who treated resistance members were also arrested.

Treatment of detained persons

The treatment of the thousands of persons arrested and detained by the Iraqis varied widely. In most cases, detained persons were first interrogated at temporary detention centres, such as police stations or school buildings and private houses which had been taken over by the Iraqi forces[11]. Many detainees were heavily beaten or severely tortured and were later transferred to a number of other detention centres for further brutal interrogations. The Juvenile Prison in Firdous, Kazima Sports Stadium, Al Mishatel experimental farm, and Nayef Palace in central Kuwait were some of the more notorious centres where inhumane and degrading treatment and torture including the rape of men and women, vicious beatings, mutilations, electrocutions, and the staging of mock-executions frequently took place[12]. It was not only those suspected of the most serious resistance activity that were treated in this barbaric manner. The torturers were frequently trawling for information in the hope that they might come up with something even remotely useful to them. One quiet-spoken, white-haired British expatriate, who had been captured in hiding in February 1991, said that the five days he spent in detention in Kuwait before being deported to Basra in Iraq were particularly horrific. He suffers to this day from the effects of the beatings and the nightmarish mock executions to which he was subjected. His only crime was that he was British and trained the horses for the Kuwaiti police force!

Money and a vast array of electrical goods including videos and televisions sometimes secured the release of the detained person; however it was more difficult to obtain a release through bribery if official papers had been filed, or there was any suspicion of resistance activity. Judges brought from Iraq to preside over sham trials[13] were also amenable to bribes. However, many people accused of being resistance members were summarily executed, and their severely tortured and violated bodies were dumped outside their homes in order to strike terror into the hearts of the local population[14]. Detainees who were neither released nor executed were subsequently transferred to Iraq.

Conditions in most of the Iraqi jails were hardly much better than those that prevailed in Kuwait. Prisoners, sometimes whole families, were moved around from camp to camp, each one just as appaling as the last. Most had been arrested in summertime and were still in the same unsuitable clothing when the remarkably cold winter arrived. There was very little water available, except what the inmates were able to buy from the guards, and food was almost non-existent. Hygiene was dreadful. One particular prison in Basra was described as a hell on earth. Each day several prisoners were removed for questioning and sounds of torture and beatings filtered through to the remaining occupants of the long, dark, dank room. There was very little light, except for a small high window, human excrement piled up on the floor, and the prisoners were covered in lice. There was not enough room for everybody to sleep stretched out at night, so they had to take turns to sit up or lie down. Many other jails were just as bad. It seems there were hundreds of places of detention ranging from police stations, regular prisons, intelligence headquarters, army and navy barracks, training camps, police colleges and even private dwellings. Nevertheless, many of them had a common denominator: they were generally filthy, overcrowded, the food was bad and distributed in small quantities at irregular intervals, there was little ventilation, poor lighting, and an absence of medical care.

Mass arrests and deportations

A third group of detainees was arrested towards the end of the conflict (19-23 February) as an ignominious defeat loomed for the Iraqis. The Iraqi security net was thrown even further afield and an order was given to detain all Kuwaiti males between the ages of 14-45. Thousands were taken, many on their way to or from early morning prayers for example. Their arrests were abrupt and unexpected; whilst some were given the reason (i.e. that they fell within the designated age-group for arbitrary arrest), others were left completely in the dark. Families waited anxiously for their menfolk to return but there was often no news and relatives were left worrying about their fate. The vast majority of those taken in this pre-retreat sweep were bundled into buses and taken to Iraqi transit camps and other detention centres further north in Iraq.

A group detained on 22/23 February was brought to transit camps near the border and other detention centres in Iraq. Again, the conditions in which they were kept were appaling. The transit camp at Abu Sakhir, which at this time held over a 1,000 captives, was particularly bad. There were four barracks in all; each one of which (30 m long by 5 m wide) was only suitable for about 50 persons but contained around 400 prisoners. Sanitation was practically non-existent; prisoners were only allowed to visit the toilets once a day in groups of five. Weakened and under pressure, they resorted to using the channel between barracks with the result that the excrement accumulated. Since water had to be collected from a polluted river some distance away, many inmates suffered from dysentery, compounding the unsanitary conditions. Food and bedding were grossly inadequate. After repeated representations, 15 small blankets were produced which had to be divided, by some miracle, between 420 prisoners! All inmates had to sleep on the cold cement floor. There was no place to pray.

A prisoner, who was also a pharmacist, was given the task of distributing what little medication the inmates received from their captors. He tried to eke out the few antibiotics, some of which had expired, to offer a limited degree of relief to those with dysentery. However, a number of people, especially those with ulcers and a prisoner suffering in excruciating pain with kidney stones, remained without medication. The pharmacist was also powerless to alleviate the suffering of a 28 year old diabetic who died a slow lingering death without the necessary insulin injections. The Iraqis were finally persuaded to send the young man to hospital but a last-minute dangerous dash by his compatriots through the rebel-controlled streets to a hospital in Basra failed to save his life.

Six hundred of those taken in the mass arrests on or about 21 February were moved from Abu Sakhir when the above group arrived, and were transported as far as al-Rashid prison in Baghdad and onto al-Mosul in the north. This is a modern prison which had been built to house Iranian prisoners of war and, although conditions were far from ideal, the Kuwaiti detainees were at least allowed to exercise in the prison grounds.

Release and repatriation

Some prisoners were released as a consequence of the uprising in the south of Iraq which followed on the Iraqi defeat in Kuwait. Jails were attacked by Iraqi rebels (Basra and Diwaniyeh jail for instance) and thrown open to release opponents of the Iraqi regime. In the ensuing confusion many Kuwaitis managed to escape. Some were undoubtedly captured by Iraqi troops, some were helped by the rebels and handed over to the Americans, others made the perilous journey back to Kuwait on foot amidst the confusion and fighting raging all around. Having survived the coalition bombing of

Basra, their greatest fear was that they would be killed in the cross-fire between the rebels and the Iraqi troops. Fortunately, many of the local population were sympathetic and helped the fleeing prisoners. Nevertheless, it was a difficult and dangerous period which called for great resourcefulness and courage.

A temporary ceasefire had been called on 27 February following the liberation of Kuwait. It was stated at the time that a permanent ceasefire would depend upon Iraq's immediate release of all coalition prisoners of war, Kuwaiti detainees and third country nationals, as well as the remains of the deceased. Iraq, in a letter to the UN Security Council, said that it would accept all the Security Council's resolutions unconditionally. Iraq also undertook to return prisoners of war to their home countries within a very short period of time. Following the meeting of military commanders at Safwan on 3 March, Iraq hurriedly freed from captivity many of those persons interned immediately prior to liberation. One thousand one hundred and eighty-two internees[15] were rushed from Abu Sakhir in a well-guarded convoy to Kuwait as a 'confidence building measure' in an attempt to reassure the allies that they meant to cooperate fully in all the matters agreed at Safwan.

Iraq had consistently refused to allow the International Committee of the Red Cross (ICRC) to visit prisoners of war and civilian internees in Iraq during the war, nevertheless, they were allowed to visit, register and arrange for the repatriation of prisoners of war and civilian internees in Iraq as soon as hostilities ceased. The first prisoners of war were handed over by the Iraqis to the ICRC in Baghdad on 4 March

---

REPATRIATIONS OF KUWAITI PRISONERS DURING MARCH 1991
9 March - registration of 1,100 Kuwaitis returning from Iraq
21 March - repatriation of 1,148 Kuwaitis from Iraq via Arar in Saudi Arabia
23 March - repatriation 1,157 Kuwaitis
25 March - repatriation of 907 Kuwaitis
26 March - repatriation of 1,149 Kuwaitis
27 March - repatriation 679 Kuwaitis*

* There were additional repatriations after this date.
From: The Gulf 1990-1991 From Crisis to Conflict, The ICRC at Work

1991[16]. The repatriation process gradually gathered momentum and by May 1991, most of the 6,909 prisoners of war and civilian internees officially[17] repatriated by Iraq in 1991 had already returned to their home countries, including 21 captured members of the ruling Kuwaiti Al-Sabah family who were released on 6 April 1991.

Missing persons

There was much joyous celebration at the return of loved ones to their friends and relatives, but it soon became clear that a considerable number of people detained by the Iraqis, many of whom had been seen in Iraqi jails, had not come home. The Iraqi Government refused to accurately account for these persons, at the same time denying, as it continues to do, that it has any Kuwaiti persons remaining in its prisons. As of 31 August 1993, the total number of files on missing military and civilian persons, formally submitted through the International Committee of the Red Cross to the Iraqi Government, was 625. The vast majority of missing persons are Kuwaiti nationals (558

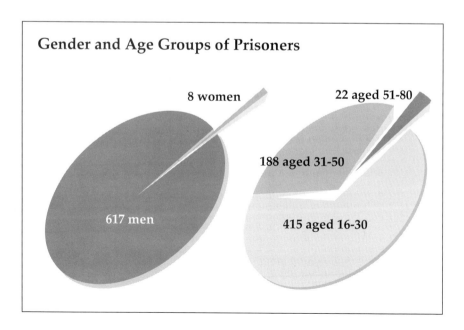

Gender and Age Groups of Prisoners

8 women

22 aged 51-80

188 aged 31-50

617 men

415 aged 16-30

males and six females). However, information was also sought by Kuwait from Iraq concerning the whereabouts of 35 foreigners (including two women) from nine nations who were sympathetic to the Kuwaiti cause: 13 Saudis, five Iranians, four Egyptians, four Syrians, three Indians, three Lebanese, and one each from Bahrain, Oman and the Philippines. Twenty-six persons of unknown nationality were also still listed as missing.

The vast majority of those released and repatriated immediately following liberation were kept in prisons, barracks and compounds in fairly large groups. It seems, on the other hand, that many of the persons reported as missing were arrested and deported to Iraq individually or in small groups and may have been swallowed up by the vast Iraqi prison system[18] and may even be registered as Iraqi nationals[19]. For this reason, it is generally believed that Kuwaiti prisoners in 'ordinary' jails in southern Iraq would still be under lock and key if they had not been set free by rebel forces. Some missing persons may even be serving prison sentences under false names since many detainees were extremely reluctant to give their own names to the authorities for fear of reprisals against relatives. Others may still be in hiding in Iraq, having escaped from custody and failed in their efforts to return home. It is clear from the testimony of ex-detainees that a number of people whom it is known escaped from prison have not yet returned to Kuwait. Some of these may have been killed in the upheaval in Iraq. Others on the list may also have died in Iraqi custody, particularly those of whom there has been no news since they disappeared. Prominent in this group may be people who were trying to cross the border to get back into Kuwait. Relatives of those who attempted border-crossings have had very little success in locating witnesses or tracing their movements following their suspected capture by the Iraqis. Regardless of the fate of missing persons, their relatives require well documented and authenticated information.

THE HUMAN TRAGEDY

One can only speculate on the physical conditions that are being experienced by Kuwaitis remaining in Iraqi jails. It does not take much imagination, however, to appreciate their mental torment. Depression, anxiety, fear, worry over their own fate, but most of all concern over the well being of family members must be their constant companions. Many are the 'head' of their individual family, husbands or eldest sons - a position which has considerable significance and responsibility in Arab society.

The relatives of missing persons are also subjected to unbearable suffering. Independent clinical studies have revealed that relatives of missing persons have a higher rate of mental anguish and trauma compared to the rest of the Kuwaiti population. Loneliness, frustration and guilt for these relatives are almost crippling in their intensity. Social life, work performance, and relationships with other family members are all impaired under the weight of this pain. Children are particularly vulnerable as their profound sorrow is mixed with the tremendous insecurity arising from the lack of information concerning their father, or, even in some instances, mother. Some relatives are working voluntarily with governmental and non-governmental organizations in the hope that they might secure the release of their loved ones. In many instances they appear to be consumed by the void in their lives and the mental gymnastics that are required to comprehend the complexities of the situation and achieve a solution. No task is too enormous or impossible, no stone is left unturned in their efforts to be reunited with family members. They have also had to learn to recognise the unscrupulous individuals who prey on their vulnerability by making unsubstantiated claims for financial gain concerning the locations of missing Kuwaitis. Sleepless nights, disrupted family life, inability to work, the impossibility of making plans for the future, or even the decisions necessary for life to continue with some semblance of normality, all take their toll.

The following stories are a small sample of the many broken and suspended lives which are a tragic legacy of Iraq's invasion and occupation of Kuwait. The family tragedies that are reported here are based upon personal interviews with close relatives that took place during a visit to Kuwait in January 1994. There are many other similar case-histories amongst the 625 files on Kuwaitis and third-country nationals reported as missing.

Sitting around the long table at the headquarters of the National Committee for Missing and POW Affairs were ten women who were patiently waiting to tell us their own sad stories. The meeting had been arranged for us by the National Committee's Director General, Duaij Al-Anazi. Our hard-working interpreter was a volunteer member of the Committee staff, Dr Rola Dashti, who works during the day at the Kuwait Institute for Scientific Research. She gives much of her free time to helping the National Committee give support to the relatives of those who are still held in Iraq. Rola had earlier explained to us that she was outside Kuwait throughout the occupation since she was studying for her Ph.D. in America. "I felt guilty that I had not done enough to help", she said. "I feel it is my duty to do what I can now to assist the families and bring back all those who the Iraqis are still holding".

We had asked for this meeting so that we could hear at first hand what the words 'POW' and 'Missing' really mean to the people whose lives were so suddenly devastated by the events following Iraq's invasion of Kuwait. Each woman held in front of her a picture of a missing loved one. They passed the pictures up to us so that we could see at close quarters the fresh-faced, well-dressed, young men and women who had been summarily taken by the Iraqis.

A mother's mission

Sitting next to us at the head of the long table was a striking woman who had made strenuous efforts to bring the issue of

The Human Tragedy

Kuwait's missing persons to the attention of the world. Pinned to her black shawl, exactly over her heart, was a photograph of her own daughter who was still held in Iraq. Before we began the interviews she brought out some large albums of pictures and slowly turned the pages. On each were several photographs of young people whose features had been recorded in happier times. Page after page of smiling young faces, each of them detained, many based on the slimmest evidence. Some were tortured and killed. Some still alive and incarcerated in Iraq's jails. None of these people had been released.

"I have made these albums for the hostages", she told us. "These are two brothers. This is my cousin, he had a camera. They took him and no one has seen him. There has been no news of him since. This is also one of our family. Also this person is from our family". Nearly all the pictures were of young men. "This is an Egyptian, his mother is Kuwaiti but his father is an Egyptian. This one is the same, mother Kuwaiti, father Egyptian. This fellow, his mother is from the United States. He was outside, in the USA, with his mother, so he came back, through Saudi Arabia, to see his family. They took him as he was passing from Saudi Arabia to Kuwait. These are also two brothers. They heard only that he is in Baghdad. This man has an Egyptian mother and a Kuwaiti father. These two and these two are brothers. This is a young Kuwaiti girl".

She continued to turn the pages, page after page of missing people. It was hard to understand how she could endure her own obvious pain let alone take on board all the distress of the many other people who were suffering a similar trauma. A woman of action, she was prepared to go to any length to ensure that the world did not forget her own missing family member, nor the other missing people. To this end she had produced posters illustrated with the photographs of several missing persons. "This is not the Government and not the National Committee", she explained. "We do it ourselves. I wanted a poster to show my own daughter's face, others wanted me to include members of their own families. Together we paid the cost of the poster. We have printed 2,000 like this and we put them up everywhere, in embassies, in schools, in every place".

Forgotten Victims

"I want you to look at these people who were killed by the Iraqis", she said. Again she turned the pages of a large photograph album in which the true horrors of Iraq's occupation were all too vividly portrayed. "This one was at the airport; this one had green eyes - what did they do? They took out his eyes.... And this one....they were all killed...not for fighting...they were simply taken in the street and killed. This is a girl also who has been killed. See, these are three brothers, they killed them all. Of course there are many more than this. This is a girl, this is a lady...they were all killed by the Iraqi soldiers without any reason. This is a girl also. Two from this family were killed by the Iraqi soldiers. This is a small boy, a baby, who was killed".

Page after page after page...the pictures continued. Every now and then the woman would stop and make sure that the horrors were sinking in. "See this one also," she told us, "he is an old man". Then the pictures changed to those of torture instruments, the electric chair and a bench full of butchering tools. We had seen them before and preferred not to look too closely or to imagine the terrible screams of the torture victims, but we could not turn away. Finally she put aside the albums and we began our interviews with the other Kuwaiti women who had come to tell us about their missing sons, daughters and husbands.

Bedr's wife's story
They came in the middle of the night when all were fast asleep. Loud banging on the door sent a shiver of fear throughout the apartment. The Iraqi soldiers who entered the Kuwaiti home on 21 November 1990 knew who they were after but when Bedr's wife begged them for an explanation they had nothing to say. Bedr's three children clung to their mother and cried, but the soldiers were carrying out their orders and forced their 28 year old father to leave with them. Ever since the invasion Bedr had feared that this might happen.

It had been hard to look after his family and he had been praying most of all that the Iraqis would not separate them. In the weeks and months since the invasion he had done his best to keep a low profile, but like many of his fellow countrymen he had been active in the distribution of food and water. His wife had begged him to be careful and he had done his best to ensure that his efforts remained undetected, but now it seemed that he had been identified as a potential threat. He may have been observed travelling around more frequently than most, or perhaps making regular visits to the same houses. The sense of fear among the Iraqis was such that they needed little excuse to arrest Kuwaitis. Not only did such arrests remove a potential adversary from the arena, they also served to spread fear among the local population. This was exactly what the occupying force wanted to achieve.

After Bedr left with the soldiers his wife telephoned his mother. What should they do? Would they torture him as they had done to so many others? The two women were frantic to secure his release. They tried to find out where he was being held but the Iraqis gave them no information. Shortly after his arrest another Kuwaiti told them that he had seen Bedr in the Juvenile Prison which was being used by the Iraqis as a holding facility. He himself had been released after a short spell there. Then they heard nothing, despite numerous efforts to obtain news of Bedr's whereabouts. Eventually however some news did come. A returned prisoner reported that he had seen and spoken with Bedr at a military hospital in Baghdad where he was being treated because he had been paralysed following severe torture. Bedr had managed to communicate his name and address to his fellow prisoner and, following his release, he had passed on the information about Bedr to his family and to the NCMPA.

Bedr's parents, his wife and children still pray daily for his return. There is not a single moment of their waking hours that they do not think of him. Like every other Kuwaiti mother or wife to whom we spoke, Bedr's mother was unable to fight back her tears as she told us her story. "We need your help," she cried. "May God help you!"

Khaled's mother's story
The next woman spoke about Khaled, her eldest son, who was

seventeen years when the Iraqis apprehended him on 20 October 1990. Still at school, Khaled was in the eleventh grade and was due to take his final examinations later that year but the invasion brought a sudden and abrupt halt to his education. He was asleep when the soldiers forced their way into his house, past his parents, and into his bedroom where they woke him and ordered him to accompany them. To this day Khaled's mother has no idea why they detained her son. The last time she saw him was in a detention centre at Ahmadi where he was held after his arrest.

A month after they took Khaled the soldiers made another frightening assault on the house, again in the middle of the night. This time they arrested the whole family, including his mother, her husband, their two and eight year old daughters, and a twelve year old son. The officer told them that they were to accompany them, that they would have to sign some forms, and that Khaled would be released immediately. Instead they were transported directly to Basra jail. Conditions were extremely tough and it was desperately difficult for Khaled's mother to care for her children. The family was split-up. The men, including the twelve year old boy, were taken to the male section and the mother, with her two daughters, was held in a female prison. "We were held in a filthy room together with many other people and left to sleep on the floor. We were given one small meal a day and only allowed one visit to the toilet". All the time they prayed that they would be reunited with Khaled whom they feared was suffering even more than themselves. From Basra jail they were moved to a number of other prisons before ending up back in the south again. The family were finally released when rebellion broke out in southern Iraq following the liberation of Kuwait.

Although Khaled's parents have received no direct news from their son in the three years since his arrest, they have met two former prisoners who confirmed that they saw him in two different prisons. The most recent reported sighting was in June 1991, eight months after his detention began, and shortly before the last official release of POWs from Iraq.

Sobhi's mother's story
Sobhi is a Lebanese national but he had lived all his life in Kuwait. He was 28 years old when, on 2 November 1990, an Iraqi officer ordered him to leave his home. He was arrested because an informer told the Iraqis that Sobhi was helping the Kuwaitis. It was easier for non-Kuwaitis to move around Kuwait at this time and Sobhi was using his comparative freedom to assist in providing food and essential supplies to his many Kuwaiti friends. The occupying forces were always suspicious that such efforts were in some way part of the resistance movement. And even the vaguest of suspicions was enough to warrant arrest and torture.

Sobhi had been running a small clothing store and was the only son in a family of seven children. His mother cried bitterly as she told us of her efforts to secure Sobhi's release. Soon after his detention he was seen by many people at the infamous Juvenile Prison. He was taken from there to Bughrabi jail where he was seen by a fellow-prisoner who has since been released. Another returned prisoner has reported seeing Sobhi in Radwaniya jail.

Daad's mother's story
Daad's brother had fallen in love with a local girl while studying in Scotland. When he completed his studies he brought her back to Kuwait. Following the invasion, the Iraqis were searching for all westerners so Daad's family had done their best to hide their British daughter-in-law. They tried desperately to contact the British Embassy to let them know that they were harbouring one of their citizens, but they were unsuccessful. They anxiously tried other embassies with the same lack of results. A Kuwaiti family did eventually give them a telephone number to call an American whom they thought might be able to help. On the same day that they were trying to make contact, 20 August 1990, the Iraqis announced that any family harbouring westerners would be arrested and executed. Needless to say, Daad's family became even more fearful. Help came in the form of a Kuwaiti resistance member who assisted Daad to hide her Scottish sister-in-law in a "safe-house". In late

October, fearing that their position had become too dangerous, Daad's mother came to where the three girls were hiding and collected her daughter-in-law to take her to another refuge. Shortly afterwards, on 1 November 1990, the Iraqis arrived at the 'safe-house' and arrested Daad and her Kuwaiti friend.

The next news of Daad came from a Lebanese man who, prior to the commencement of the air war on 17 January 1991, reported that he had seen Daad in Iraq. He knew her since they had both been held in the Juvenile Prison in Kuwait and had been taken together on the same bus to Iraq. The family have also received information that Daad was being held in Radwaniya jail. Her mother's face was etched by the pain and suffering, but she remains full of hope that her daughter will be released from her imprisonment and return to Kuwait.

Fahad and Shaheen

Fahad and Shaheen are twin Kuwaiti boys. They were 23 years old when they were arrested on 21 October 1990. The Iraqis raided the house at eight o'clock in the morning. Only three of the five boys in the family were in the house at the time because their mother had separated them in the expectation that the Iraqis would search their house one day, as they had done to so many others. Fahad and Shaheen were arrested but their 13 year old brother was left alone. No reason was given for their arrest. Ten days later their father was detained. After four months he was returned to his family, but he had severe mental problems as a result of the torture he had endured during his captivity. The people detained with him said that he was victimised because he was constantly asking about his sons. "Where are my sons, what have you done with them?" he would demand. The Iraqis regularly took him away and tortured him as punishment for his outspokenness. Other prisoners heard his screams and, each time, there would eventually be silence. Each time he was returned to his cell, his fellow-prisoners were convinced that he would die but he always recovered. The torture was repeated so often that his mind was affected.

After the liberation a Lebanese who was an ex-prisoner was shopping for a car and spoke of his experiences in detention to the car salesman. The twins' mother heard the story and made contact with the Lebanese man through the car salesman. She showed him pictures of her sons and he told her that he had been held with them in Bughrabi jail. He did not know the names of the two boys but recognised them from their photographs. He apologised to her for having to tell her that they were both extremely thin when he last saw them, however, this was one of the things that convinced their mother that his information was accurate since her two sons had always been exceptionally thin. The boys' mother looked at us in despair; "We are not liars"! she cried. "Where did our children go? This is the truth. May God help us. Now I am with their father who has lost his memory, who does not know what has happened? How can I manage? And what about Shaheen's wife? He got married on the Wednesday before the invasion. She was only with him for a short time, now she does not know what to do with her life. She is undergoing psychological treatment".

Bedr's wife's story
Bedr's wife brought her youngest daughter with her to the interview. She was three years old when her father was captured and is now six. He had been a sergeant in the Kuwaiti army, but had retired before the invasion. However, on the day of the invasion his brother came to their house to tell him about the advancing Iraqi army. Bedr put on his military uniform and left the house. That was the last that his wife or any of his colleagues saw him. There are no reports of sightings in any detention centres or jails. He was 37 years old when he disappeared. Bedr's wife and five children are left wondering whether he is alive or dead. His youngest daughter clung to her mother and sobbed uncontrollably as we spoke of her father. Like many children who are the youngest in the family, she was her father's pet and cannot understand what has happened to him.

Marzouk's mother's story
Marzouk was 35 years old, married, with four children when he was taken on 25 September 1990. The oldest boy is 12 years

old and the youngest child, a girl, was born on 25 August 1990. Marzouk was an aircraft engineer in Kuwait Airways. He had previously served in the military forces but was no longer doing so at the time of his arrest. At around two in the morning, the housekeeper came to their bedroom and told them to wake up because Iraqi soldiers were going to search the house. Marzouk's wife was still very weak after childbirth and subsequent hospital treatment, but the soldiers insisted that everyone should leave the house. As soon as they were all outside on the road, the soldiers began firing at the house. There were around 50 soldiers present. They indicated that they were arresting Marzouk. His mother pleaded with the soldiers to let her son go. "Why are you taking him?" she asked them. "You will find out later", the officer replied.

The next day Marzouk's mother went in search of her son, travelling from jail to detention centre, to jail, hoping to glean some information. Finally, she went back to one of the jails which she had already visited and the Iraqi guards admitted that they held Marzouk and that he had been arrested because of his military connections. After much pleading they brought her to see him. He had been severely tortured and was covered with blood. He was unable to walk. She returned the following day to see him but they refused her entry. The next day she went back again, but this time they denied that he was ever there. The same happened on the following day. Eventually she persuaded an Iraqi officer to tell her that her son had been moved to the Juvenile Prison. She went there and was refused permission to see him because he was being held in isolation. The soldiers told her that if she wanted to bring him food and clothes that she could do so, but she could not see him. She returned home, picked up clothes and food for him and returned to the jail. "Please let me see my son, even from a distance", she begged them. "I don't even need to talk to him if you will let me see him", but the Iraqis refused.

Eventually a prisoner who had been released from the Juvenile Prison came to Marzouk's mother to give her news of her son. "I was with Marzouk in the Prison", he told her. "He was surviving but was always complaining about his mind.

The torture seems to have affected his brain", he explained. His mother never gave up. She kept returning to the Juvenile Prison asking to see Marzouk. Eventually one of the people there told her that some of the prisoners had been moved to Jahra jail. Marzouk's mother travelled to Jahra, and searched the whole area. Although she could not get concrete proof that he was there, she explained that she felt sure that he was in Jahra. When the air war began prisoners held at Jahra were taken to Basra. Later she spoke to two prisoners who were released from Basra jail who said that they had seen Marzouk there. After liberation two released prisoners stated that they had seen Marzouk in Bughrabi jail, close to Baghdad.

Marzouk has only spent one month with his youngest child. She, for her part, reflecting her mother's anguish, constantly asks when the father she does not remember will return.

Safi's mother's story

Safi was 18 years old when he was captured. Later, the Iraqis arrested his whole family, separating the male and female members from one another. His mother and sisters were, like many other detainees, moved around from jail to jail; from Basra to Diwaniyeh to Al Daghgharah and then back to Diwaniyeh. Safi's little sister almost died. She was suffering from anaemia and there was no medical treatment available. The effects of imprisonment in such harsh conditions have had a long-lasting effect on her young mind. Her nights are broken by horrible nightmares, even though the light in her bedroom burns brightly and her family make sure that one of them hugs her tightly for reassurance.

The women and children were eventually released and repatriated through Saudi Arabia to Kuwait, with the help of the allies; but they still did not know whether their father and Safi were safe. Safi's father eventually returned home having been set free when the rebels in southern Iraq threw open the doors of Basra jail. But there was no news of Safi, although the Lebanese ex-prisoner who saw Fahad and Shaheen, the twin boys, also saw Safi in jail. His little sister, along with the rest of the family wait anxiously for some news.

Abdel Razzak

Abdel Razzak was in Syria when the invasion took place. Aged 22, he was the eldest son and he felt his place was with his family in Kuwait. He travelled first to Saudi Arabia and, on 6 November 1990, he attempted to cross the border into Kuwait. He was apparently captured near the border and has not been heard of since. Throughout the occupation Abdel Razzak's mother presumed he was safe outside Kuwait, staying perhaps with cousins in Saudi Arabia. After liberation, she contacted these cousins and inquired about her son. "He should be with you", they told her. "We left him at the border". It later became clear that he had been held for around two months at the Juvenile Prison in Kuwait and he was then taken to Amarah jail in southern Iraq. A Lebanese man released in June 1991 reported to the family that he had seen Abdel Razzak at a special detention centre in a converted villa in Iraq. Abdel Razzak's parents are sure that their son is alive in Iraq's jails and work diligently for his release.

Bedr's mother's story

Bedr was captured on the 26 October 1990 at the age of 26. A member of the police force with the responsibility for guarding Kuwaiti Airlines, he was at home when he received a telephone call from his boss asking him to come and see him at his house. When he arrived he found that the call was part of an Iraqi trap which had already captured several other people, not all of whom were involved in the security or military forces. Three days after Bedr was captured his mother received a telephone call from one of his friends who explained that he had seen Bedr, that he was in good health, and that they should stay calm.

Six days after Bedr's capture an Iraqi soldier called his mother, he would not say where he was being held but simply that he was alright. He also called Bedr's sister and gave the same story. Presumably these calls were at Bedr's request. Then the Iraqi soldier demanded video cassettes, radios and other gifts as a bribe to get Bedr released. Rather than meet the soldier at their home, they decided to do so at a cafe in the centre of town. "The gifts are not for me", the soldier told them, "they are for my officer". Two days later they had an appointment with him and paid him what he had demanded. They did not hear from him until one month later when he called back to say: "unfortunately Bedr was not included in the group that we have just released, but he will be with either the second group or the third group". A number of reliable sources subsequently confirmed that Bedr had been in a detention camp in Kuwait. There was one gentleman who was working with Bedr, who knew him very well, and who saw him and confirmed that he was certainly surviving his ordeal up to the time when he was taken to Baghdad in January 1991. A Kuwaiti airline captain who was captured and later released, and who knew Bedr, made a definite statement that he was there until the move to Iraq. Prisoners who returned to Kuwait from Baghdad claimed to have seen him in prison in Baghdad up to February 1991. The last news of him coincided with the latest releases from Iraqi prisons.

Samira's mother's story

Samira, born on 24 July 1964, was a third year student at Kuwait University's Faculty of Commerce. On the morning of the invasion she told her mother that she would go to Mubarak Hospital to lend assistance. "Be careful!" her mother told her. "Don't worry Mum", she replied, "I know what I am doing". Everything seemed to be fine, until 9 November when she came home at three o'clock in the afternoon. She had her lunch with her mother and left. "I will call you at five o'clock", she promised. "I will be here", her mother replied, but Samira did not call at five o'clock and at five-thirty her mother felt that something was wrong. "Everyone was talking to me and I was very short-tempered. Then, that night I tried to call her. She gave me several telephone numbers. I tried to call her everywhere, but nobody answered. Then, after 11 pm I called her flat and an Iraqi soldier answered. I put down the phone. I tried again to call her again the next day, but with no luck. Nobody could help me".

Two weeks passed before definite news of Samira's arrest at

a checkpoint was given to her mother. Then, on Christmas night, more than a month after she had disappeared, her mother received a telephone call from a woman who said that she was calling on behalf of Samira, who was still "o.k." and who would be home in a few days. Samira's mother promised the woman anything she wanted if her information was correct, but the caller said she did not want anything and that it was dangerous to talk on the telephone.

On the same day a man telephoned and said that he had a letter from Samira. He would not say where she was being detained but promised to bring the letter the following day at one o'clock in the afternoon, at a pre-arranged meeting place. The letter was duly collected and Samira wrote that she was in reasonable health, but could not say where she was. "I will be home after two or three days", she wrote. Her sister-in-law had been due to deliver a baby soon after Samira was arrested and she asked if it was a boy or a girl. She also asked for some food and clothes which were duly delivered via the intermediary. All in all the family had about six or seven letters from Samira in one week. Samira told her mother in these letters that the Iraqis had not harmed her, but had used her to write letters and send faxes to Baghdad. At her own request, her family sent her money and more food and clothes.

Nothing more was heard until the 4 January 1991, when an Iraqi lady who was married to a Kuwaiti called and said that she was phoning on Samira's behalf. She said that Samira might be released after a few days but that she needed more food and clothes. She asked her mother to cook something special for her. Her mother cooked *machbous*-rice with meat. Samira's mother accompanied the Iraqi woman with the food to the Juvenile Prison. The woman said it would be safer for Samira and her mother if she did not enter the jail. The Iraqi woman then went inside and returned with two letters from Samira. Samira wrote in one of them that she was about to be transferred to Basra.

The two women waited in the car outside the prison with the Iraqi woman hiding on the floor. Samira's mother waited anxiously to catch a glimpse of her daughter who eventually emerged in the company of another detainee. Samira's mother followed the car for a short distance in which her daughter and companion were driven away, but she was afraid to go too close in case the Iraqis would see the tears streaming down her face. Samira managed a small wave of farewell and that was the last time her mother saw her.

In June 1991, a man telephoned and said he had been in jail with Samira in Baghdad and that she would probably be free in one or two months. He described her as being very thin and pale with longish black hair, but that she was in good mental condition. He said that she sent her regards to her parents who were not to worry about her because she was alright. He also said that there were two or three other girls with her where she was held at Qasimiah jail, a female prison in Baghdad.

There was no more news until August 1991. A doctor friend of Samira's mother telephoned from Jordan late one night. She explained that an Egyptian acquaintance of her Jordanian husband had been released from jail in Iraq and that he had heard Samira's name spoken outside the gates of his jail. The ex-detainee had explained that when he had been near the gates of the jail, he had seen many women and girls covered with black *abayas*. He had no way of knowing if Samira was actually with them but he claimed to have definitely heard her name spoken.

A lady also called and claimed that she had been with Samira for three days in Ba'qooba jail in March 1992, and that she was in reasonable health. She said that shortly after that, the guards were taking them in a bus to Saddam Palace, but that Iraqi dissidents captured the bus and released them and that they were repatriated with the help of the ICRC. Next a Lebanese man came to the family claiming to have seen Samira. He confirmed that it was actually her he had seen from a photograph Samira's mother showed him, and explained that she had been with him for eight hours in a bus from Abu Ghraib jail to al-Ramadi jail. He stated that there had been six girls together but when they had entered the jail, the girls had been split off from the men. He had been taken to a section where people were registered with the ICRC and subsequently released, but he did not see Samira again.

Samira's mother has heard from many people who said that Samira had been with them in jail, but it is over a year since she has received any concrete news about her daughter. Other sources of information have indicated that Samira is being held with Daad, the Lebanese girls whose story is recounted above. Samira is reported to have an injured leg and Daad is apparently taking care of her.

Samira's mother pleaded: "We do not know anything and we really need your help. It is three years and three months since my daughter was taken. What happened? What can we do? Where can we go for help?"

The case of Faisal 'Abd Al-Hamid 'Abd Al-Aziz 'Abd Al-Hamid Al-Sane and relatives:
The following case history which has been compiled from interviews and sources other than those described above, is just one more example of the many missing persons whose arrest and detention by the Iraqis has been well-documented. The National Committee for Missing and POW Affairs has carefully compiled detailed files on 625 persons. Amnesty International has also produced a report which includes the case histories of 140, and the photographs of 120, missing people[1]. Such cases are presently being used to bring pressure on Iraq to answer questions concerning missing Kuwaitis.

Faisal Al-Sane, married with four children, was a member of Kuwait's National Assembly who had graduated from Baghdad University in 1964. He was a well known Kuwaiti businessman who lived in the al-Kifan district of Kuwait city and it was there, on 21 September 1990, that he was arrested at his *diwaniyah* (traditional Kuwaiti meeting place attached to his private house), together with a group of male relatives and friends who were present at the time. It is believed that the Iraqis had been trying to persuade Faisal Al-Sane to give active support to their occupation of Kuwait, but that he had consistently refused to do so. Recently the authorisation forms and other Iraqi documentation in connection with these arrests have been produced by Kuwait sources as positive evidence that Faisal Al-Sane was detained by the Iraqis. Whilst such written evidence may have helped to convince some poorly informed Iraqi officials and diplomats, it was hardly necessary to convince people in Kuwait since the events surrounding the arrest of this group were already very well known. After their arrest Faisal Al-Sane and his colleagues were all taken to Basra and most were subsequently released, including Faisal's son Ziad. Still missing, are Faisal's nephew Khaled, a human rights activist (who was last reported by a released prisoner who saw him at al-Fudailiyya Prison in Baghdad in June 1991); Nasser 'Abd Al-Majid 'Abd Al-Hamid Al-Sane who graduated from Cairo University in 1968, where he studied journalism, and 'Abd Al-'Aziz Sa'ud 'Abd Al-'Aziz Al-Sane who was studying commerce and was just over 20 years old when arrested.

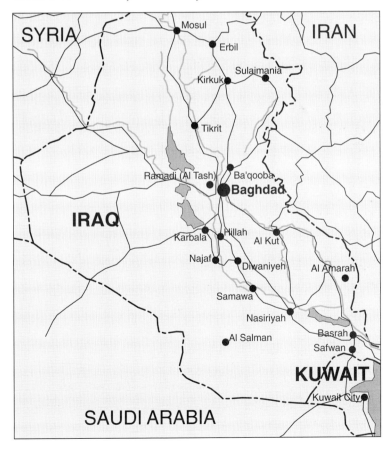

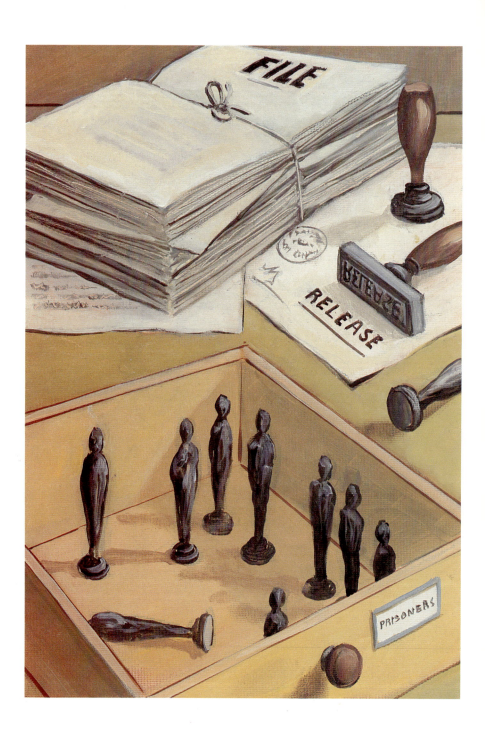

EFFORTS TO RELEASE THE PRISONERS

Kuwaiti organisations

Kuwait's efforts to ensure that all Kuwaiti and third country nationals arrested by Iraq during its occupation would be released started as early as December 1990, during the occupation of Kuwait. It was then that the Kuwait Human Rights Committee was established in Saudi Arabia in order to collect the names of people who were detained by the Iraqis. An initial list of more than 11,000 names was prepared, but because of the practical difficulties associated with compiling such a list during the occupation without the cooperation of Iraq, and the lack of experience of Kuwaiti officials in these matters, that first list, submitted to Iraq in April 1991, contained numerous inaccuracies. Many names, for example, appeared several times within the list. One of the problems was that Arabic names can have a number of variations and different versions of the same name were frequently added to the list. In addition, many Kuwaitis were afraid to give their real name when they were arrested. After giving a false name they could be trapped by that misleading identification[1] since they were afraid of the many spies and informers within the Iraqi prison-system.

The National Committee for Missing and POW Affairs (NCMPA)

The National Committee for Missing and POW Affairs (NCMPA) was officially established by the Kuwaiti Government on 5 May 1991[2]. It was clear by that stage that although over 6,500 Kuwaitis had been released and repatriated in March/April 1991, not all persons detained by the Iraqis had returned home. Therefore, the NCMPA, in addition to its role in coordinating efforts to relieve the physical and mental distress and ensure the financial security of the relatives of missing persons, was entrusted with the initial task of establishing and completing files on all Kuwaiti missing persons so that the Iraqi Government could be formally approached about the issue. There was, however, a general feeling that the problem would be solved very quickly by itself: that Kuwait's allies in conjunction with the Security Council would be able to make Iraq comply with all Security Council resolutions, which included the demand that all prisoners of war and civilian detainees be released[3]. There was a strong belief therefore that all missing persons would be returned home very soon. It took some time for those involved in the issue to realise that they were in for a long hard battle of an entirely different kind to the one that had just ended.

A Special Rapporteur appointed by the UN Human Rights Commission was informed by the NCMPA in June 1991 that over 3,800 persons were missing following the occupation of Kuwait. By late September 1991 the official list of missing persons contained 2,443 names and was under constant review by the Kuwaiti authorities as new information came to light, duplicated names were removed from the list, and families were reunited with missing members. Names were also omitted from the new list because their cases were no longer considered to be of direct concern to the Government of Kuwait[4].

The UN Special Rapporteur later received another list from the NCMPA, dated 13 October 1991, which contained the names of 2,101 missing persons[5]. Unfortunately, not all the inaccuracies had been eliminated. Because of the complete mistrust between the two countries, Iraq refused to believe that the mistakes made in the listings of missing persons were due to administrative difficulties and problems of data gathering in the difficult situation which followed liberation, and were not primarily aimed at disparaging Iraq's attempts to comply with Security Council resolutions. It skilfully used the inconsistencies to discredit the Kuwaiti claim that its citizens were still detained in Iraqi jails. By March 1992, the Kuwaiti list had been reduced to 850 people.

Kuwait, for its part, acknowledges that genuine mistakes were made because they did not have the expertise or the manpower to carry out a proper investigation. In addition, the failure of Iraq to issue lists of prisoners, or allow the ICRC access to prisoners of war or detainees during the conflict, meant that official records were practically non-existent. The point is made that if Kuwait had wished to add to the list of missing persons in order to discredit Iraq, it would have falsified names rather than duplicated them. The NCMPA points to the considerable efforts that have now taken place to ensure that the most recent information submitted to the Iraqi Government on detailed forms, the prototype of which was drawn up by a special tripartite sub-commission[6], is absolutely authentic, has been scientifically collected, and is altogether verifiable within the confines of the subject matter. Iraqi documents, including arrest sheets, left behind after the hasty retreat from Kuwait, have been scrutinised, and relatives and other witnesses, including ex-detainees who have seen the listed persons in detention in Iraq, have been carefully questioned. The NCMPA are particularly grateful to the ICRC who trained researchers in the painstaking task of collating all available information. A significant improvement in the efficiency of the NCMPA was also made when a senior executive of the Kuwait Oil Company was seconded as Director General of the National Committee in July 1992. His organizational expertise, gleaned from 20 years of business experience, has proved invaluable.

Carefully completed files on 625[7] missing individuals were handed over to the Iraqi Government, with the help of the ICRC, at several different times in 1992 and 1993. In the meantime, as well as taking care of the welfare of relatives, the NCMPA, aided by committed volunteers, works tirelessly at the international level actively seeing information on, and the release of, all missing persons.

Kuwait Association for the Defence of War Victims (KADW)
In addition to the efforts expended by the NCMPA, a non- governmental organisation, the Kuwait Association for the Defence of War Victims, is also endeavouring to use its good offices in search of concrete information concerning the whereabouts of missing persons, and to secure the release and repatriation of those still detained. Members of this organization, some of

them ex-detainees or relatives of missing persons, have devoted much time, energy and money to the difficult task. They have travelled widely using all their available resources in order to highlight the humanitarian aspects of the problem and are careful to stress that the question is not one of numbers but of individuals, and that those individuals must not be the unwilling pawns in any political game. Disavowing any interest in politics nationally or internationally, they wish to work for the release of prisoners in a similar manner to the intercessions made by mediators on behalf of western hostages in Iraq in 1990, even though this means that they leave themselves open to criticism that they may appear to consort with the enemy. Criticism of this nature emanates from uncompromising individuals who do not wish to give Saddam Hussein even the remotest acknowledgement that he may be in a position to still inflict suffering on the Kuwaiti nation. Unfortunately, at the present time, the Iraqi leader is probably the only one capable of resolving the problem.

International pressure

Kuwaiti governmental and non-governmental organizations, including the Kuwait Lawyers Association, as well as influential Kuwaiti citizens have lobbied intensely in order to place the issue of missing persons high on the agenda in the international arena. Appeals for help in solving this problem have been made, amongst others, to many Arab Governments, individually and through the Arab League, to the US Congress, to the European Union, the UK House of Parliament, the French Government, and to the Non-aligned Movement; but the most significant international forum for dealing with the issue has been the United Nations.

United Nations

The United Nations has been active on the issue of missing persons since the liberation of Kuwait. In particular, the Security Council has adopted a number of pertinent resolutions. Directly after the cessation of hostilities, Security Council resolution 686 (1991), 2 March 1991, ordered Iraq to:

"[i]mmediately release under the auspices of the International Committee of the Red Cross, Red Cross Societies, or Red Crescent Societies, all Kuwaiti and third country nationals detained by Iraq and return the remains of any deceased Kuwaiti and third country nationals so detained"[8].

It further demanded that Iraq:

"arrange for immediate access to and release of all prisoners of war under the auspices of the International Committee of the Red Cross and return the remains of any deceased personnel of the forces of Kuwait and the Member States cooperating with Kuwait pursuant to resolution 678 (1990)"[9].

As already indicated Iraq complied to a certain extent with this demand. Nevertheless, resolution 687 (1991) of 3 April 1991, noted "that despite the progress being made in fulfiling the obligations of resolution 686 (1991), many Kuwaiti and third country nationals are still not accounted for...". Paragraph 30 of the same resolution therefore ordered Iraq to:

"extend all necessary cooperation to the International Committee of the Red Cross, providing lists of such persons, facilitating the access of the International Committee of the Red Cross to all such persons wherever located or detained and facilitating the search by the International Committee of the Red Cross for those Kuwaiti and third country nationals still unaccounted for"[10].

Resolution 687 also declared that the Council would review the sanctions on Iraq, in place since 6 August 1990, every 60 days "in the light of the policies and practices of the Government of Iraq, including the implementation of all relevant resolutions of the Security Council for the purpose of determining whether to reduce or lift the prohibitions referred to therein"[11]. The repatriation and release of Kuwaiti and third country nationals, as well as information concerning those who may have died in custody or elsewhere, is an important element of this review process[12].

Unfortunately, little progress was made on the missing persons issue, prompting the Security Council to adopt resolution

706 (1991), 15 August 1991, which underlined its concern "that the repatriation or return of all Kuwaitis and third country nationals or their remains present in Iraq on or after 2 August 1990, pursuant to paragraph 2(c) of resolution 686 (1991) and paragraphs 30 and 31 of resolution 687 (1991)" had not yet been fully carried out[13].

A letter dated 2 January 1992, from Iraq's Permanent Mission to the United Nations at Geneva, addressed to the Centre for Human Rights[14], set forth Iraq's position with regard to the release of Kuwaiti detainees. It claimed that Kuwait had mounted a media campaign on this issue with the aim of prolonging the "unjust economic embargo and sanctions against the Iraqi people" and stated that Iraq had "meticulously fulfiled the commitments contained in paragraphs 30 and 31 of Security Council resolution 687 (1991)". Furthermore, the Iraqi letter went on to state that "[Iraq] has also cooperated fully with the International Committee of the Red Cross by submitting lists of the Kuwaitis in Iraq, which helped to facilitate the registration of Kuwaitis and other foreign nationals and the repatriation of all Kuwaiti subjects approved by the competent Kuwaiti authorities..."

The letter also reported on a mission by representatives of the League of Arab States to Iraq; and on a number of lists handed by the Iraqi authorities to the League's Secretary General. These lists claim that 6,943 Kuwaitis were repatriated from Iraq through the ICRC as of 9 October 1991 and that 3,711 Kuwaitis registered by the mission of the ICRC at Baghdad were awaiting approval from the Kuwaiti authorities for their return to Kuwait[15]. The Iraqi letter stated that the "competent Iraqi authorities currently have no information" regarding "remaining people on the Kuwaiti list" and that their apparent disappearances "may be attributable to three possible reasons:

(a) A number of them may be living in Iraq with their relatives and may have failed to register their names with the mission of the International Committee of the Red Cross in preparation for their return to Kuwait;

(b) During the incidents in Kuwait, many Kuwaitis were on summer holiday in Europe, America, South-East Asia and elsewhere. It is therefore possible that many of these may have not yet returned to Kuwait and are living and pursuing their various activities in those countries;

(c) Many Iraqi and Kuwaiti civilians killed either in Kuwait or in Iraqi territory as a result of the bombing of Kuwait and Iraq by aircraft belonging to the coalition countries".

Obviously, Kuwaitis could have been killed in either Kuwait or Iraq during the war, however, the Iraqi explanations ignored the fact that the Kuwaiti list of October 1991 was composed solely on the basis of information registered with the NCMPA by close family members[16] who would surely be aware if their missing family members were still abroad, either with relatives in Iraq or elsewhere.

A few weeks later a letter from the Charge d'affaires a.i. of the Permanent Mission of Iraq to the United Nations addressed to the President of the Security Council, on 23 January 1992, said in relation to compliance with paragraph 30 of resolution 687 (1991) that on 17 December 1991, the Iraqi Ministry of Foreign Affairs had submitted a request to the ICRC mission in Baghdad in which the Ministry proposed that the ICRC prepare a complete implementation plan, to be agreed upon between Iraq and the coalition countries, for measures to be adopted in the search for Kuwaiti, Saudi, Iraqi and other nationals still missing, in accordance with the provisions of the Geneva Convention of 1949. The letter of 23 January 1992 again pointed to the considerable number of Kuwaitis and other nationals that had been repatriated by Iraq in March/April of 1991, and to the numbers of persons living freely in Iraq who had submitted requests through the ICRC to return to Kuwait. Iraq therefore claimed that it had implemented its commitments to facilitate the repatriation of all Kuwaiti and third country nationals carefully and in earnest[17], that it was cooperating fully with the United Nations in relation to all its obligations under resolution 687, and again claimed that the continued imposition of the sanctions against Iraq was a purely political stand adopted by certain States Members of the Security Council.

Iraq's assertions of total compliance with the relevant UN resolutions are not supported by the Secretary-General's report to the Security Council of 25 January 1992. Attached to this report is a letter from the President of the ICRC[18] who agreed that the ICRC had registered about 3,700 persons in Iraq whose nationality could not be established with certainty. These persons claimed that they had been living in Kuwait and expressed their wish to return to their former place of residence. The ICRC had transmitted information to Kuwait who was processing applications[19]. The ICRC also stressed that the Kuwaiti authorities had insisted that the names of persons on that list were not included on the list of missing persons compiled by Kuwait. The ICRC emphasised that it had not received any information as to the whereabouts of the persons reported missing in Iraq. Nor had it received detailed and documented information on the search conducted by the Iraqi authorities. It was also awaiting information on persons who had died while in custody. The ICRC pointed out that no agreement was reached between representatives of the coalition forces and the Iraqi Government on the methods to be adopted in the search for missing persons[20]. In the absence of this agreement, the ICRC was powerless to act.

Whilst the Secretary-General's report agreed that much had been achieved as regards Iraq's compliance with UN resolutions, it was clearly stated that much remained to be done. The report also painted a graphic picture of the cat-and-mouse games which the Iraqi authorities were playing with the UN[21]. The comments of the Director-General of the International Atomic Energy Agency (IAEA) on Iraq's compliance with its obligations in relation to nuclear activities sums up the matter very succinctly. He claimed that the Iraqis consistently denied clandestine activities until the evidence was overwhelming. This denial was followed by cooperation until the next case of concealment was revealed. Unfortunately, it was and is very difficult to produce overwhelming evidence of the presence of Kuwaiti prisoners in Iraqi jails without compromising vulnerable sources or without Iraq's full cooperation

In a further letter dated 28 February 1992, the Minister for

Foreign Affairs of Iraq again insisted that Iraq had extended all necessary cooperation to the ICRC in implementation of the provisions of paragraph 30. This was disputed by former members of the coalition who claimed that the Iraqi letter was "an attempt by Iraq to delay fulfiling its commitments under the Geneva Conventions and the relevant Security Council resolution"[22]. They stated that although Iraq's letter referred to its preparedness to take certain steps, Iraq had yet to comply. A number of UN delegations (including those of France, UK, the Russian Federation, Cape Verde and Zimbabwe) also expressed their dissatisfaction with Iraq's efforts at this time. The French delegation in particular said that once again Iraq had deliberately delayed any meaningful cooperation on that issue, displaying a totally callous and uncooperative attitude towards the plight of the missing and the suffering of their relatives[23].

Tariq Aziz, the Iraqi Foreign Minister, was moved to respond thus:

> "Why should Iraq do this thing? What benefit could it expect to gain from detaining one or two thousand Kuwaiti citizens when Iraq had already repatriated high-ranking Kuwaiti officers and other high officials, including 20 members of the ruling family in Kuwait?"

He said once again that Iraq had requested on 20 February that the whole matter be entrusted to the ICRC.

The UN Commission on Human Rights was also concerned with the delay in releasing and repatriating prisoners of war and detained civilians in the context of general violations of human rights in Kuwait during the Iraqi occupation. It addressed the issue in a resolution in March 1991[24] and again in March 1992, having appointed a Special Rapporteur, Walter Kälin, to draw up a report on human rights abuses during the occupation[25]. The Commission resolution[26], expressing its deep concern at the grave violations of human rights and fundamental freedoms during the occupation of Kuwait, also noted with grave concern "the continued detention of prisoners of war and civilians abducted from Kuwait and the refusal of Iraq to account for the whereabouts of these detainees". It strongly condemned "the failure of Iraq to treat all prisoners of war and detained civilians in accordance with the internationally recognised principles of humanitarian law" and insisted that "it refrain from subjecting them to acts of violence, including ill-treatment, torture and summary execution". It requested:

"the Government of Iraq to provide full information on all Kuwaiti persons and third-country nationals abducted from Kuwait between 2 August 1990 and 26 February 1991 who may still be detained, and to free these persons without delay, in accordance with its obligations under article 118 of the Geneva Convention relative to Prisoners of War and article 134 of the Geneva Convention relative to the Protection of Civilian Persons in Time of War and its obligations under applicable Security Council resolutions".

It also requested:

"the Government of Iraq to provide, in accordance with its obligations under articles 120 and 121 of the Geneva Convention relative to Prisoners of War and articles 129 and 130 of the Geneva Convention relative to the Protection of Civilians Persons in Time of War, detailed information on persons arrested in Kuwait between 2 August 1990 and 26 February 1991 who may have died during or after that period while in detention, as well as on the location of their graves".

It further requested:

"the Government of Iraq to search for the persons still missing and to cooperate fully with international humanitarian organizations such as the International Committee of the Red Cross, in this regard";

and it demanded that:

"the Government of Iraq cooperate with and facilitate the work of international humanitarian organizations, notably the International Committee of the Red Cross, in their search for and eventual repatriation of Kuwaiti and third-country nationals detained and missing in Iraq".

The UN Commission on Human Rights also alluded in 1992 to the plight of missing persons in a resolution[27] which strongly condemned "massive violations of human rights in Iraq"[28], calling on the "Government of Iraq to release immediately all persons arbitrarily detained, including Kuwaitis and nationals of other States".

The President of the Security Council issued a statement on the situation between Iraq and Kuwait at its 3139th meeting on 23 November 1992 at which he stated:

> "In spite of ICRC's best ongoing efforts, ICRC has not received information as to the whereabouts of the persons reported missing in Iraq. Nor has it received detailed and documented information on the search conducted by the Iraqi authorities...ICRC has still not received permission to visit Iraqi prisons and detention centres in accordance with standard ICRC criteria. Very few missing persons/detainees have been released since March 1992, while hundreds are believed still to be inside Iraq".

The Secretary General used the occasion to reassert that:

> "..the Security Council insists that it [Iraq] allow immediate access by international humanitarian organizations to all those in need of assistance in all parts of Iraq, and demands its cooperation with the Secretary General to these ends."

In concluding remarks on this general assessment of Iraq's compliance with its obligations, the Secretary General stated that "the Security Council has considered itself justified in concluding that Iraq has up to now only selectively and then partially complied with the obligations placed upon it by the Council".

In December 1992[29] the UN General Assembly called upon the Government of Iraq to release immediately all persons arbitrarily arrested and detained, including Kuwaitis and nationals of other States. Iraq meanwhile continued to deny the existence of such prisoners, deflecting attention by a skilful criticism of Kuwait's humanitarian efforts on the issue of Kuwaiti missing persons[30]. Iraq drew heavily upon reported criticism of these efforts made within the Kuwait National Assembly, by a parliamentary committee established to examine the issue, claiming that this committee's report stated that:

"the procedure of the Kuwaiti authorities has been characterised by inconsistency and clumsiness and by an attempt to exploit the issue of missing persons for political purposes. That has resulted in a weakening of the issue's credibility in all international forums and at the governmental and non-governmental levels".

Summarising the various claims that had been made upon it for the return of missing people, the Iraqi Permanent Representative to the UN informed the Secretary-General that in their opinion the most eloquent proof of the inconsistency of the allegations launched by the Kuwaiti authorities was the numbers cited in the lists of missing persons submitted by those authorities to Iraq through the ICRC. During the period from March 1991 to March 1992, Iraq said that Kuwait had submitted seven lists with completely different figures[31]. Iraq concluded that:

"The exposure of the tendentious political goals on which the allegations of the rulers of Kuwait were based and their inconsistency in submitting seven random lists assists greatly in bringing forth the truth and opening the way for closure of the file on section G of Security Council resolution 687 (1991), particularly since the information came from inside Kuwait".

Iraq conveniently ignored the fact that the Kuwaiti parliamentary committee, whilst highlighting the inefficient way in which the lists were handled by the authorities, did not in any way arrive at the same conclusion as Iraq. The committee is as convinced as the Kuwaiti authorities that Kuwaiti nationals detained by Iraq during the occupation are still being held in Iraq, and that the file can by no means be concluded on this matter. In fact some members of the parliamentary committee were themselves detained in Iraq during the occupation and are personally acquainted with many of the people on the missing persons list. Iraq continued to claim that it was doing everything possible to solve the issue, as it had indicated at numerous international forums, but failed to acknowledge that the conditions it had placed upon its cooperation made it impossible for ICRC to undertake its task.

Iraq, in May and June of 1993, asserted that the release and repatriation to Kuwait by Iraqi authorities, through the ICRC, of six Kuwaiti brothers, a month after they were arrested by an Iraqi soldier close to Kuwait's border with Iraq, was further evidence that it did not have any Kuwaiti detainees and certainly had no interest in holding on to Kuwaitis[32]. "This responsible humanitarian action proves the spuriousness of the fabricated allegations of the existence of Kuwaiti detainees in Iraq. It is also proof of Iraq's true and sincere intention of cooperation on such humanitarian issues", it claimed.

Kuwait did not accept the Iraqi assertion[33] and pointed out that Iraq had neglected to mention that it was still detaining a number of third country nationals who had lost their way or who were taken forcibly in the demilitarized zone. Kuwait also underlined that such cases were dealt with by the Kuwaiti side in a manner which bore no relationship to prisoners or detainees. Such was the case when Kuwait, on 5 May, returned seven Iraqi children sighted the previous day by a Kuwaiti patrol on the Kuwaiti side of the demilitarized zone between Umm Qasr and Safwan. Kuwait later claimed[34] that no progress whatsoever had been made on the issue of Kuwait's missing persons in the two years which had passed since the adoption of resolution 687 (1991). It laid the blame for the lack of progress firmly at Iraq's door stating that Iraq had not cooperated with the ICRC on the matter, nor had it made any response to the presentation by the ICRC, many months previously, of 627 detailed files, despite the fact that the ICRC had specifically requested a reply and that Iraq had responded to other queries within 10 days. Kuwait also pointed out that Iraq had declined to receive an emissary of the Secretary-General of the League of Arab States, Mr Rashid Idris, who wished to travel to Iraq to extend his good offices as an intermediary for the release of prisoners and detainees[35]. It had also "thwarted the efforts of the Moroccan monarch, King Hassan II" in his effort to secure the release of Kuwaiti prisoners and detainees.

In the period between July and November 1993 there continued to be virtually no progress on the issue as letters from Kuwait to the Security Council[36],very much along the lines of those quoted above, attest. Kuwait continued to protest the fact that many months later, Iraq had still not responded to the 627 files presented by the ICRC and it criticised Iraq's continued refusal to attend the meetings of the tripartite committee (comprising coalition members, Iraq and the ICRC) dealing with the issue of prisoners, detainees and missing persons, (meetings of which had been convened by the ICRC in Geneva in July and October 1993).

Kuwait's case was strengthened by the issuing of a report by Amnesty International on 8 September 1993[37] in which the independent organization stated that "there is strong evidence to suggest that many people arrested by Iraqi forces during the occupation, and who were subsequently transferred to Iraq, are still being held".

Kuwait also drew attention to Iraq's proposal for establishment of a committee to include Morocco, Qatar and members of the Kuwaiti Parliament "to conclude this matter, by directly investigating the facts" and submitted that this was both an acknowledgement by Iraq of the existence of prisoners and detainees and an effort to further confuse the issue by overlapping and by-passing the Security Council resolutions and the ICRC efforts. Whilst welcoming any effort "that would assist in resolving this humanitarian question", Kuwait affirmed that such efforts should be "within the framework of the will of the international community as reflected in Security Council resolution 687 (1991) and all other relevant resolutions".

The latest review (January 1994) of Iraq's compliance with relevant UN Security Council resolutions has not brought any new information to light.

International Committee of the Red Cross

Having been refused any meaningful role in the protection of prisoners of war and civilian internees during the war, the ICRC, on 7 March 1991, sponsored the setting up of the tripartite committee in Riyadh, Saudi Arabia composed of Iraq and the coalition forces. The purpose of the committee was to define repatriation procedures for prisoners of war and detainees on both sides of the conflict. A second and third round of Iraqi/coalition talks were held under the auspices of the ICRC on 21 and 28 March 1991. By this stage most of the nearly 7,000 persons, prisoners of war and civilians, repatriated from Iraq to their home countries were already on their way to be reunited with their families. Therefore the main topic of the commission was the speeding-up of the repatriation process for the many thousands of Iraqi prisoners of war held in Saudi Arabia. It was agreed, however, at the third round of Riyadh talks to establish a sub-commission on missing cases. This sub-commission subsequently met in Geneva on 16 and 17 October 1991 to discuss methods and operational procedures for achieving, in the shortest possible time, tangible results in the search for and repatriation of persons reported missing by both Saudi Arabia and Kuwait.

Iraq agreed to publish the names of missing persons in one Iraqi newspaper. It also said it was willing to provide the ICRC with a list of prisons and places of detention in order to facilitate ICRC visits to these places. The visits were to be restricted to one per site. The sole objective of the visits was to be the search for Kuwaiti and Saudi missing persons. Iraq also requested that the principle of reciprocity be applied, namely that the same procedures would be applied also in Kuwait and Saudi Arabia[38].

Representatives of the coalition forces, responding to the ICRC on 21 November 1991, expressed dissatisfaction with the Iraqi approach. Firstly, because they considered that publication in only one Iraqi newspaper was insufficient. Secondly, they objected to ICRC visits being limited to one per site. Thirdly, they objected to reciprocity being the basis for further action. The Iraqi Ministry of Foreign Affairs reiterated its previous position to the ICRC on 17 December 1991, and invited the ICRC to prepare a plan containing methods and procedures for the tracing of missing Kuwaiti, Saudi, Iraqi or other nationals in accordance with the Geneva Conventions.

Unfortunately, the ICRC has not been able to visit jails, detention centres or prison camps in Iraq because of the conditions laid down by Iraq for such visits. The ICRC will only undertake visits to prisoners of war or political detainees if they are in a position to visit all places of detention where prisoners are held; if they are permitted to interview all detainees in private; and if they are able to make repeat visits. They make the point that unless such conditions are permitted their visits serve no humanitarian purpose and could be used for propaganda[39]. In stark contrast to the restrictions placed on it in Iraq, the ICRC has had complete access to Kuwaiti jails. Under its protection mandate it has been able to visit Palestinians, Jordanians and Iraqis sentenced by the State security court as well other nationals. The ICRC asserts that Kuwait cooperates fully with its requirements with regard to visits to prisons in Kuwait.

One positive early development by the tripartite sub-commission mentioned above was the drawing up of a standard form which Kuwait has been able to use to document its case to Iraq concerning missing persons. As already explained, the ICRC has been of enormous help to Kuwait in collating records and filling out this standard form and whilst it is not their role to vet the information on the forms, they have provided some assistance in cross-checking and ensuring that the missing persons files were as well prepared as possible, under the difficult circumstances that prevailed. In the view of the deputy director of the International Committee of the Red Cross delegation in Kuwait, the submitted forms present a credible case for Kuwait's missing persons, but he points out that this may not be the full picture. In fact the total number of missing persons may be greater since the ICRC in Kuwait has been approached by some people searching for lost relatives who, for their own reasons, have not submitted names to the Kuwaiti National Committee, or whose missing relatives have not been accepted for inclusion on the official Kuwaiti list.

As the UN report indicated, the tripartite sub-commission met twice in 1993, but this time without any Iraqi representation which essentially emasculates its effectiveness. The ICRC to date has not received any detailed and documented information on any search conducted by the Iraqi authorities and they are ready at any time to allow people to convene and facilitate any movement towards a resolution of the problem.

LEGAL BACKGROUND

Introduction

This chapter will briefly examine the legal background to Iraq's treatment of the inhabitants of Kuwait during its occupation of Kuwaiti territory. Since its main purpose is to lead to a better understanding of the plight of missing persons in Iraq, it concentrates almost exclusively on issues relating to arrest and detention.

The old adage *inter armes silent leges* (law is silent during war) is not technically accurate. Although the outbreak of war is frequently marked by a breakdown of domestic law and order, theoretically an international legal regime which is designed to blunt the savagery of war comes into force when hostilities erupt. This regime, whose ancient roots are firmly implanted in most of the world's great moral and cultural traditions, has become known in recent times as international humanitarian law. Admittedly, many commentators are particularly sceptical about the relevance of international humanitarian law to modern warfare, especially in the light of recent atrocities such as those committed against the civilian population in parts of the former Yugoslavia. However, a lengthy discussion on the futility of efforts to humanise war is beyond the scope of this chapter. It is sufficient to say at this point that unnecessary suffering and perverse cruelty, whilst morally reprehensible, are also militarily ineffective since they distract fighting men from their central task which is the efficient utilization of military force in pursuit of victory. In any case States have come together to negotiate a number of international treaties that contain legal prohibitions against such inhumane behaviour.

The main international treaties codifying the rules governing the waging of war between States which are of immediate concern are: the Regulations annexed to Hague Convention IV of

1907; the Geneva Conventions of 1949, and Protocol I additional to the Geneva Conventions, which was adopted in 1977. Iraq is a party to the four Geneva Conventions but not to the Hague Regulations or to the Additional Protocol. Kuwait, for its part, has ratified the four Geneva Conventions and the Additional Protocol but not the Hague Regulations. The fact that the Protocol applies only between States which are parties[1] meant that it was not formally applicable during the armed conflict between Iraq and Kuwait. However, even though States are only bound by treaties which they have ratified or acceded to, they are also obliged to conform to the rules of customary international law: a body of unwritten law which has evolved through customary practice reinforced by the opinion of States that such customs are legally binding. In some instances customary rules have been codified in treaties, or treaty rules have become universally accepted and form part of customary law. The Regulations annexed to Hague Convention IV of 1907 are considered to be part of customary international law, so too are some provisions in Additional Protocol I of 1977.

The law governing the conduct of war (*jus in bello*) is not fundamentally linked to the law on the use of force (*jus ad bellum*) which outlaws the waging of aggressive war. Once a conflict erupts, international humanitarian law does not adjudicate on the lawfulness of the use of force, neither does it distinguish between the aggressor and the defender: the law of war applies to all the parties to the conflict without discrimination. In particular, the fact that Iraq was in breach of international law by waging an unlawful aggressive war did not release Kuwait from its obligations under that law. However, in practice it may be argued that a more stringent interpretation of military necessity is imposed on the aggressor.

Because modern international law outlaws the waging of aggressive war, it also has declared unlawful the acquisition of territory by the use of force, even if the aggressor believes it has sovereign rights over such territory. Shortly after the invasion, Iraq annexed Kuwait[2], claimed it as part of its nineteenth province, and refused at all times to recognise that it was in occupation of Kuwaiti territory. This kind of unilateral annexation is not legally effective as was underlined by UN Security Council Resolutions 662 and 664[3]. It is clear therefore that title to Kuwaiti territory remained at all times with the legitimate Kuwaiti sovereign. The law simply recognised Iraq as the belligerent occupant who was temporarily administering the territory in place of the Kuwaiti sovereign. As occupant, once it had gained effective control of Kuwaiti territory[4], Iraq was obliged to restore public order and safety to Kuwait, "while respecting unless absolutely prevented, the laws in force in the country"[5].

International humanitarian law is not the only international legal regime which is in force during armed conflict. Human rights treaties, although primarily formulated to regulate the peacetime relationship between a government and its people, are also applicable during hostilities. In particular Iraq, as party to the International Covenant on Civil and Political Rights, was obliged at a very minimum to abide by the non-derogable provisions[6] of that treaty[7].

Legal protection for prisoners of war

The laws of war presume that the inhabitants of a State at war fall into two distinct categories, civilians and soldiers. The third and fourth Geneva Conventions of 1949, which were in force from the time Iraq crossed the border into Kuwait on 2 August 1990[8], broadly reflect this categorization. The third Convention deals with the treatment of prisoners of war, and the fourth with the protection of civilians.

Traditionally, only members of the regular armed forces of a State were entitled to participate directly in military operations, i.e. be classed as 'lawful' combatants, and they were the only ones legally entitled to prisoner of war status on capture. However, the third Convention expanded the category of persons entitled to combatant and prisoner of war status[9] to organized resistance movements, operating in or out of occupied territory[10], who belong to a party to the conflict[11]; are commanded by a person responsible for his subordinates; are readily identifiable by a fixed distinctive sign recognisable at a distance; who carry their arms openly; and who conduct their operations in accordance with the laws and customs of war.

The third Convention, in line with tradition, also makes some allowance for the spontaneous uprising of the civilian population against an invading force before that force has actually taken control. Members of a civilian *levee en masse* (as such a spontaneous uprising is called) are also entitled to combatant and prisoner of war status, as long as they carry arms openly and conduct their operations in accordance with the laws and customs of war. Once the occupant has taken control, individual armed resistance is not considered to be lawful.

The rules on combatancy and prisoner of war status were relaxed in Additional Protocol I of 1977 to take account of the realities of modern warfare. Under that treaty all combatants, including members of organized resistance movements of a party to the conflict who are subject to an internal disciplinary system which shall enforce compliance with the rules of international humanitarian law[12], are, as always, required to distinguish themselves from the civilian population in order to prevent accidental targeting of innocent civilians. However the requirement to wear a fixed distinctive sign and the carrying of arms openly, especially in military operations in occupied territory where such conditions could mean that all armed resistance would be rendered impossible, have been transformed into the single requirement that a combatant must carry arms openly:

(a) during each military engagement, and

(b) during such time as he is visible to the adversary while he is engaged in a military deployment preceding the launching of an attack in which he is to participate[13].

As already stated, Iraq has not ratified Additional Protocol I, and since the modified criteria for combatant and prisoner of war status in that treaty are not universally considered to be part of customary international law, they were probably not formally applicable in the Kuwait-Iraq conflict. Nonetheless, it is particularly ironic that most Arab countries at the diplomatic conference which negotiated Additional Protocol I argued vehemently for the modification in the traditional criteria for granting combatant and prisoner of war status. The harsh reali-

ty is that without the benefit of the rules contained in Additional Protocol I, persons other than those in the regular armed forces, or members of organized resistance movements fulfilling the restrictive conditions outlined in the third Geneva Convention, are not entitled to prisoner of war status but are deemed to be civilians and may be held to be criminally liable for the act of bearing arms.

Members of the Kuwaiti armed forces who were resisting the invasion were targeted and killed by the Iraqis. Despite the illegality of the use of force by Iraq, since the *jus ad bellum* and the *jus in bello* are separate, it could be argued that such killings constituted legitimate acts of war. Most of the members of the Kuwaiti armed forces who were captured by the Iraqis during the invasion and the occupation were entitled to, and seem to have been granted, prisoner of war status[14] and were subsequently interned in Iraq. The third Geneva Convention permits the removal of prisoners of war for internment in the territory of the belligerent State[15].

There is no record of any member of the resistance movement being recognised as having combatant or prisoner of war status. Neither is there any record of a competent tribunal meeting to decide the matter[16]. The question of whether resistance members fulfilled the conditions which would have determined their eligibility for such status is difficult to assess without further study. In any case, as already underlined, only a small number of persons who were resisting Iraqi occupation were involved in active resistance, a smaller number again were involved in armed violence.

The third Geneva Convention sets down stringent conditions for the treatment of prisoners of war. Responsibility for such treatment lies at all times with the Detaining Power[17]. The Convention declares that:

"[p]risoners of war must at all times be humanely treated. Any unlawful act or omission by the Detaining Power causing death or seriously endangering the health of a prisoner of war in its custody is prohibited, and will be regarded as a serious breach of the present Convention"[18].

In addition Article 17 states that no physical or mental torture, nor any other form of coercion, may be inflicted on prisoners of war to secure from them information of any kind whatever. Prisoners of war who refuse to answer may not be threatened, insulted, or exposed to any unpleasant or disadvantageous treatment of any kind.

The Iraqi authorities did eventually make some effort to comply with the broad thrust of the third Convention by keeping most of the prisoners of war in camps where conditions were considerably better than in other places of detention. However, all the many and detailed provisions of the Convention were certainly not adhered to. It was particularly unfortunate that delegates from the ICRC were not allowed to visit and register Kuwaiti prisoners of war in Iraq during hostilities[19]. Neither was an Information Bureau for prisoners of war, as required by Article 122 of the Convention, established by Iraq. If either one of these obligations had been carried out, the eliciting of information concerning missing prisoners of war would have been made considerably easier

Iraq cooperated in the release and repatriation of most prisoners of war at the close of hostilities in line with Article 118 of the third Convention. However, it seems that it has not released and repatriated all those who were entitled to prisoner of war status. According to Article 5, the third Geneva Convention applies to prisoners of war "from the time they fall into the power of the enemy and until their final release and repatriation". The fact that the war may have ended does not mean that protection ceases. Neither are prisoners of war permitted under any circumstance to "renounce in part of or in entirety the rights secured to them by the Convention"[20]. Therefore, any persons still detained by the Iraqis who may be entitled to prisoner of war status[21] remains under the protection of the Convention. If any such prisoners died whilst detained[22], Iraq is obliged to issue death certificates showing particulars of identity, the date and place of death, the cause of death, the date and place of burial and all particulars necessary to identify the graves[23]. In addition, all particulars of burials and graves should have been recorded with a Graves Registration Service established by Iraq.

Legal protection for civilians in occupied territory

During the occupation, the inhabitants of Kuwait, other than prisoners of war protected by the third Convention, were entitled to the protection of the fourth Geneva Convention. This Convention, entitled the Civilians Convention, applies almost exclusively to a special category of "protected persons". These are deemed to be persons who "at a given moment and in any manner whatsoever, find themselves, in case of a conflict or occupation, in the hands of a Party to the conflict or Occupying Power of which they are not nationals"[24]. All Kuwaitis, foreigners, and stateless persons who were long-term residents of Kuwait were therefore subject to the protection of the Civilians Convention[25]. 'Protected persons' deported to Iraq also retained that status.

As already stated, once an occupying power is in control of territory it must retain the law of the true sovereign[26], but it has the power to "subject the population of the occupied territory to provisions which are essential to enable the Occupying Power to fulfil its obligations" under the fourth Convention, in order "to maintain the orderly government of the territory, and to ensure the security of the Occupying Power, of the members and property of the occupying forces or administration, and likewise of the establishments and lines of communication used by them"[27]. This is not a licence to enact any or all laws. In fact, severe limitations are placed on the authority of the occupying power. Iraqi penal provisions promulgated during the occupation, such as the amalgamation of the Kuwaiti and Iraqi court system and other institutions, the abolition of Kuwaiti money, the compulsory display of Iraqi car licence plates and the compulsory procurement of Iraqi identity cards were clearly unlawful. So too were efforts to force Kuwait nationals to pledge allegiance to Saddam Hussein[28], and to suppress genuine efforts to distribute food and money to the needy. Efforts to force civil servants to return to work were also unlawful[29]. Most importantly, the right to ensure the security of Iraqi forces did not extend to the vicious terrorization of the civilian population at large on the mere suspicion that some of its members may be involved in activity prejudicial to the security of the occupier. There is little doubt that the Iraqi occupying force far exceeded the limited authority it had to restore law and order, as is obvious from its drastic response to even the most harmless display of disaffection from the Kuwaiti population.

It is clear from evidence presented in previous chapters that Iraq also breached many basic provisions of the fourth Convention in its treatment of the inhabitants of Kuwait, both in terms of its treatment of the population at large (including women and children), and those who were detained as a result of arrests and searches. The following is a non-exhaustive list of some of the more fundamental provisions which were violated. The Iraqi authorities contravened Article 27 which entitles protected persons, in all circumstances, to respect for their persons[30] and, their honour, their family rights, their religious convictions and practices, and their manners and customs, and declares that they must be treated humanely at all times, "especially against all acts of violence or threats thereof and against insults and public curiosity", and protects women against any attack on their honour, in particular rape, enforced prostitution, or any form of indecent assault. Iraq also breached Article 31 which categorically prohibits all forms of coercion against protected persons; Article 32 which prohibits corporal punishment, torture or any other measures of brutality against protected persons; Article 33 which prohibits collective penalties and reprisals against protected persons and their property; Article 34 which prohibits the taking of hostages; and Article 28 which prohibits the use of protected persons to render strategic sites immune for military operations.

The fourth Geneva Convention, under certain restrictive conditions, entitles the authority in occupation to intern protected persons. However, as the UN Special Rapporteur investigating violations of human rights in Kuwait during the occupation affirmed, the mass, arbitrary or prolonged detention of civilians perpetrated by the Iraqis was not justified, even in terms of military necessity, and in many cases was not in conformity with the procedures set out in Article 78 of the fourth Convention. In addition, the deportation of civilians to Iraq violated the prohibition under Article 49 of the Convention of the transfer and deportation of civilians from the occupied territory to the territory of the occupying power. The dreadful conditions under which protected persons were detained also breached practically every single regulation for the treatment of internees in the fourth Convention[31].

Resistance under occupation may be considered a patriotic duty by most people, nonetheless, under the fourth Convention, the occupiers are legally entitled to protect themselves against serious resistance activity. Therefore certain penal provisions enacted by Iraq in Kuwait to protect its forces could have been permissible under the fourth Convention, for example, that prohibiting the possession of weapons[32]. However, the threat of execution, and the implementation of that threat for such an offence, was certainly not lawful. Article 66 permits the trial in non-political military courts for breach of penal provisions enacted by the occupying power to ensure its security, but courts must sit in occupied territory. Most importantly, Article 67 states that "[t]he courts shall apply only those provisions of law which were applicable prior to the offence, and which are in accordance with general principles of law, in particular the principle that the penalty shall be proportioned to the offence. They shall take into consideration the fact that the accused is not a national of the Occupying Power".

Article 68 provides that:

> "[p]rotected persons who commit an offence which is solely intended to harm the Occupying Power, but which does not constitute an attempt on the life or limb of members of the occupying forces or administration, nor a grave collective danger, nor seriously damage the property of the occupying forces or administration or the installations used by them shall be liable to internment or simple imprisonment, provided the duration of such internment or imprisonment is proportionate to the offence committed".

Article 68 also allows for the death sentence for persons guilty of:

> "espionage, or serious acts of sabotage against the military installations of the Occupying Power or of intentional

offences which have caused the death of one or more persons, provided that such offences were punishable by death under the law of the occupied territory in force before the occupation began".

Nevertheless, all persons so accused must have a fair trial. It is not at all clear that Iraq complied with any of these provisions. Executions were frequently summary, and according to the UN Special Rapporteur, "where trials took place they did not comply with the relevant fundamental guarantees of fair trial, including those applicable in times of war". In particular, it seems that sentences were not proportionate to the offences, and that the proper notification process for the carrying out of death sentences was not adhered to. The Rapporteur concludes that the "evidence indicates that executions in public or in front of families and the exposure of dead bodies in public were carried out for the purpose of spreading terror among the civilian population". In addition, inhumane treatment, including torture was systematically meted out to those even vaguely suspected of offering resistance, contrary to fundamental prohibitions contained in the Geneva Conventions, the International Covenant on Civil and Political Rights and the norms of customary international law[33].

Iraq also breached Article 76 of the fourth Convention which states that:

> "[p]rotected persons accused of offences shall be detained in the occupied country, and if convicted they shall serve their sentences therein. They shall, if possible, be separated from other detainees and shall enjoy conditions of food and hygiene which will be sufficient to keep them in good health, and which will be at least equal to those obtaining in prisons in the occupied country. ... Protected persons who are detained shall have the right to be visited by delegates of the Protecting Power and of the International Committee of the Red Cross, in accordance with the provisions of Article 143".

The latter article provides that:

> "Representative or delegates of the Protecting Powers shall have permission to go to all places where protected persons are, particularly to places of internment, deten-

tion and work.

They shall have access to all premises occupied by protected persons and shall be able to interview the latter without witnesses, personally or through an interpreter.

Such visits may not be prohibited except for reasons of imperative military necessity, and then only as an exceptional and temporary measure. Their duration and frequency shall not be restricted.

Such representatives and delegates shall have full liberty to select the places they wish to visit...

The delegates of the International Committee of the Red Cross shall also enjoy the above prerogatives. The appointment of such delegates shall be submitted to the approval of the Power governing the territories where they will carry out their duties".

Unfortunately, Iraq did not allow the ICRC access to protected persons detained in either Iraq or Kuwait. This decision could not be justified on the basis of imperative military necessity. If the ICRC had been able to make such visits Iraq might have been restrained, in its treatment of the inhabitants of Kuwait, from contravening practically every single provision of the fourth Geneva Convention.

Under the fourth Geneva Convention, the Iraqi authorities were obliged to facilitate the repatriation of civilian internees as soon as possible after the close of hostilities[34]. Many civilian internees were returned to Kuwait. However, there is strong evidence to support the Kuwaiti assertion that a significant number of civilians arrested by Iraqi forces during the occupation, and who were subsequently transferred to Iraq, are still in detention in Iraq in contravention of the fourth Convention. Article 77 states that "[p]rotected persons who have been accused of offences or convicted by the courts in occupied territory, shall be handed over at the close of occupation, with the relevant records, to the authorities of the liberated territory". According to Article 6 protected persons who have not been repatriated are still entitled to the protection of that Convention even though hostilities have officially ceased[35]. The fourth Convention also provides that "[b]y agreement between the

Detaining Power and the Powers concerned, committees may be set up after the close of hostilities, or of the occupation of territories, to search for dispersed internees"[36].

The tripartite commission composed of coalition members, Iraq and the ICRC, set up in March 1991 is one such committee envisaged by the fourth Convention. Unfortunately, Iraq has declined to attend the most recent meetings of the subcommission and without their full and genuine cooperation it is difficult to proceed in any meaningful manner.

The task of such a committee would have been made much easier if Iraq had complied with the provisions of the fourth Convention which seek to ensure that proper records are kept of interned protected persons. For example compliance with Article 106, which provided for the transmittal of an internment card to a Central Tracing Agency, would have helped considerably in the search for missing persons. Iraq was also obliged under Article 129 to certify the deaths of all internees, and under Article 130 to "forward lists of graves of deceased internees to the Powers on whom the deceased internees depended, through the Information Bureaux provided for in Article 136". Such lists must include all particulars necessary for the identification of the deceased internees, as well as the exact location of their graves. Article 131 called for an official enquiry following the death or serious injury of an internee.

None of the above obligations were carried out by Iraq, nevertheless, a properly functioning committee with full authority to search for missing persons may be the only hope for the release of Kuwaiti and third country nationals detained by Iraq following the occupation of Kuwait. It is vital that the matter should not be delayed interminably while political wrangling takes place. Time may be running out for detainees. Amnesty International fears that many Kuwaitis and third country nationals who remain in detention in Iraq have been subjected to torture and that others may have been extrajudicially executed or died as a result of the conditions of their imprisonment, and that the risks of such treatment continuing are high[37].

CONCLUSIONS

There is considerable evidence that a significant number of people, forcibly detained by Iraq during the occupation of Kuwait and illegally deported to Iraq, are still incarcerated in Iraqi jails. The horrific treatment meted out to former Kuwaiti detainees before their release, as well as the continuing reports of massive violations of human rights in Iraq, give much cause for concern regarding these prisoners. Others, listed as missing following the occupation, may be dead; some may even be in hiding in Iraq. The human tragedy, both in terms of prisoners who are suffering untold misery, and the relatives of missing persons who are enduring severe mental anguish because they have been denied information concerning the whereabouts of their loved ones, is enormous.

The Iraqi Government refuses to respond to Kuwaiti requests for information in relation to the files of 625 missing persons which were submitted to it early in 1993. It officially denies at every opportunity that it has Kuwaiti or third country nationals in its jails. Iraq also refuses to cooperate meaningfully with the ICRC or other bodies in the search for missing persons, despite the fact that the removal of sanctions is linked to the implementaion of UN Security Council resolutions which require Iraq to provide such cooperation.

Iraq's reluctance to respond adequately to the humanitarian problem with which it is faced appears to be primarily based on its belief that the issue is a political fabrication orchestrated by a vindictive opponent in order to further discredit its efforts at compliance with Security Council resolutions. In the climate of mistrust that prevails, it has sought to exploit the difficulties experienced by Kuwait in compiling an accurate list of missing persons. But it is now clear that Kuwait has worked very hard to ensure that the most recent list is accompanied by as much corroborating evidence as possible, given the inherent difficulties in providing the necessary proof.

Conclusions

It has become virtually impossible for Iraq to continue to claim that it has no knowledge of many of the people on the Kuwaiti list. At a very minimum, it is legally obliged to guarantee humane treatment to all those that it is holding, whether prisoners of war or civilians; provide information about the legal basis for their arrest and detention; and allow the ICRC, their families and lawyers access to them. Prisoners of war are also unequivocally entitled to be released and repatriated, as are Kuwaiti and third country civilians who were illegally deported to Iraq and detained without the benefit of due process for reasons that have long since ceased to be relevant. Iraq must also make genuine efforts to facilitate the search for missing persons whose whereabouts are not known, and, if deaths have taken place, efforts must be made to provide reliable verification and return the remains of the deceased to their relatives.

To help achieve full and meaningful cooperation, Iraq should attend and participate fully in the meetings of the tripartite commission which was set up under the Geneva Conventions in order to implement the search for missing persons. Nevertheless, to ensure success without untoward delay, all the members of the tripatite commission must show an inherent flexibility and a political maturity in their dealings with Iraq.

Further international pressure from Arab Governments and others will be required to help solve the impasse that has arisen, and to encourage Iraq to recognize that the issue of missing persons is a live humanitarian one and not just a political football to be deflected with meaningless rhetoric. In the years since the liberation of Kuwait, other horrific wars have attracted international attention and brought even more tragic consequences for still more innocent victims. The consensus may be that the issue of missing persons is one that Kuwait will have to live with like many other countries recovering from the effects of war. Although understandable this cynical approach is not acceptable to the Kuwaiti people including the relatives of the missing persons who are legally and morally entitled to have their loved ones returned to them.

INTRODUCTION

[1] Official figures as of August 1993. Third State nationals from nine nations sympathetic to the Kuwaitis during the occupation are also missing; 13 Saudis, five Iranian, four Egyptians, four Syrians, three Indians and one each from Bahrain, Oman, and the Philippines. In addition 26 people of unknown nationality are listed as missing.

[2] The International Committee of the Red Cross refers to these people simply as 'missing persons' since Iraq continues to deny that it is still holding any Kuwaiti 'prisoners of war'. Indeed the term 'prisoner of war' can be misleading in itself. Even though a person may be imprisoned by the enemy during war-time, he or she may not be properly called a 'prisoner of war'. The entitlement to the legal status of 'prisoner of war ' (or POW for short) is strictly controlled by the third Geneva Convention of 1949 which guarantees humane treatment to such prisoners. That Convention declares that only members of the armed forces of a party to the conflict, including members of militia or volunteer corps which form part of those armed forces, as well as some civilian personnel accompanying the armed forces, are entitled to prisoner of war status. However, members of organized resistance movements can qualify for prisoner of war status if they fulfil certain restrictive conditions, as explained in the chapter on the legal background to arrests and detentions during the occupation. Persons detained by the enemy who fall outside these categories, although imprisoned during war, should be referred to as civilian detainees or internees.

ARREST AND DETENTION

[1] See *Report on the situation of human rights in Kuwait under Iraqi occupation*, prepared by Mr. Walter Kälin, Special Rapporteur of the Commission on Human Rights, in accordance with Commission resolution 1991/67. UN doc. E/CN.4/1992/26, p.20. However, it seems that some may have been arbitrarily executed. The Special Rapporteur received information from a Kuwaiti police investigator who participated in armed defence during the first days of the invasion and was captured with two colleagues by Iraqi military forces after a shooting incident. He reported that shortly after their apprehension one of them was shot in front of him by Iraqi military personnel when they refused to answer questions concerning their military activities. (Ibid., p.34).

[2] The number rose from 638 after the first couple of days of the invasion to 678 towards the end.

[3] Many Kuwaitis were abroad on holidays when the invasion commenced. Others managed to flee across the border into Saudi Arabia in the early days of the occupation. Border crossings were subsequently closed, however, at a later stage the Nusweib border post was opened for Kuwaitis to cross into Saudi Arabia. Approximately 200,000 Kuwaitis out of a pre-occupation total of approximately 826,586 remained in Kuwait during the entire occupation. According to estimates of the Kuwaiti Central Statistics Administration, the rest of the population of 2,142,600 before the occupation included 1,316,014 non-Kuwaitis. Among the non-Kuwaitis were an unknown number of stateless persons (also known as bidoun - literally without) who were long-term residents of Kuwait possessing a special status with limited rights, as well as a considerable number of expatriate workers. Many foreigners managed to flee the country, most of them under the most horrendous conditions, but European and American nationals were detained by the Iraqis.

[4] Government-supported supermarkets in which the residents of the area in which they are situated own shares.

[5] See report of the UN Special Rapporteur cited in footnote 1 above,p.26.

[6] For example, Kuwaiti courts were "affiliated to the chairmanship" of the Basra Court of Appeal (Statement No. 5853 of the Minister of Justice of 1 September 1990), published in *Alwaqai Aliraqiya* (the official gazetteer of the Republic of Iraq), vol. 33, No.41, 10 October 1990, p.3. The Kuwaiti dinar, which had earlier been declared at parity with the Iraqi dinar, was abolished on 26 September 1990 (Revolutionary Command Council resolution No 383 of 6th Rabii'Al - Awwal, 1411 H./25 September 1990), published in *Alwaqai Aliraqiya*, vol.33, No.41, 10 October 1990, p.2. Kuwaiti establishments and organizations were also dissolved and their properties and rights were incorporated into Iraqi administrative structures.

[7] A news-sheet handed out at supermarkets on 12 September 1990, listed 10 such orders. The Iraqi-sponsored newspaper, published in Kuwait, *Al Nida'a* which was in operation until the press was broken-up and shipped away just before liberation - also published occupation orders along with Iraqi propaganda.

[8] Initially Kuwaiti dinars were used. When Saddam Hussein abolished the Kuwaiti dinar, Iraqi dinars were supplied instead.

[9] Europeans and Americans in Kuwait were rounded up and moved from Kuwait to Iraq

as early as 6 August. Iraq closed all borders to foreigners attempting to leave Iraq or Kuwait on 9 August, however Arab and non-European workers were still permitted to leave, albeit under horrific conditions. Further deportations of foreign nationals from Kuwait to Iraq took place on 16 August and by 17 August 1990 it was clear that approximately 10,000 detained foreign nationals from selected countries were being held by Iraq as hostages. Offers were made by Iraq to release all those detained in exchange for a US withdrawal from the Gulf region and an end to the blockade which had been imposed on Iraq. The majority of western women and children were allowed to leave Baghdad at the beginning of September 1990, however a number of hostages were deployed to strategic sites around Iraq. Saddam Hussein ordered the release of all western hostages in Iraq and Kuwait on 6 December 1990.

10 Resolution of the Iraqi Revolutionary Command, No. 341 of 3rd Safar 1411 H./24 August 1990, published in *Alwaqai Aliraqiya* vol.33, No.37, 12 September 1990, p.3.

11 Many cases of torture were reported from Sabah al Salem, Jahra, Hawalli, Farwaniya, Salmiya and Firdous police stations. Some schools, including Abdallah Mubarak and Abdallah Salem secondary schools were also said to serve as torture and detention centres.

12 The report of the UN Special Rapporteur, cited in footnote 1 above, includes extensive information regarding torture and cruel, inhuman and degrading treatment by Iraqi occupying forces. See especially pages 27-31. Extensive studies on torture during the occupation have also been carried out by Kuwaiti and Danish specialists at the Al-Riggae Specialized Centre in Kuwait. See in particular studies carried out by Dr Abdullah Al-Hammadi and also the report prepared by Allan Staehr, Mia Staehr, Jaafar Behbehani and Soren Bojholm, *Treatment of war victims in the Middle East*, International Rehabilitation Council for Torture Victims (1993).

13 The report of the UN Special Rapporteur, cited at note 1 above, includes some reference to abbreviated judicial procedures to which some detainees were subjected, see in particular p. 36.

14 See in particular report of the UN Special Rapporteur cited at note 1 above, at p.35.

15 This is the number arrived at by members of the group who had striven to keep an accurate register of all detainees at the Abu Sakhir camp. The ICRC met this group at the border and their official figure is 1,176.

16 Ten POWs (six Americans, three British and one Italian) were taken by road to Amman in Jordan.

17 6,698 of these were repatriated to Kuwait, including 4,233 prisoners of war and 1,291 civilians. The balance is made up by the 1,174 internees who were released from the Abu Sakhir camp and who were returned to Kuwait via Safwan before they could be registered by the ICRC. The total number also includes 81 civilians and two Kuwaiti prisoners of war and two civilians returned at the end of 1991.

18 The *Report of the Special Rapporteur on Human Rights in Iraq* (UN doc. E/CN.4/1992/31, 18 February 1992) noted that information and testimonies that he had received revealed the use of all sorts of centres of detention, with over 100 places having been identified by witnesses. He claimed that this information was in stark contrast to the Government's contention that there are at present only four functioning prisons in Iraq. The Special Rapporteur continued:
"In Iraq, neither is the due process of law generally respected nor is the rule of law upheld. On the contrary, information and testimony received reveals a consistent if not routine failure to respect due process. At the same time, and perhaps partly because of it, the rule of law has been completely undermined"(p. 66).

19 Indeed Iraq, in defiance of the UN, continues to refer to Kuwait as the 'Governorate of Kuwait', implying that it is a part of Iraq.

THE HUMAN TRAGEDY
1 Amnesty International AI Index: MDE 14/05/93: Iraq: Secret detention of Kuwaitis and third country nationals.

EFFORTS TO RELEASE THE PRISONERS
1 Because of difficulties with identifying missing people by name, photographs have been used for identification purposes in the files and reports submitted to the Iraqi authorities.

2 The National Committee, which is headed by Sheikh Salem Al-Sabah, was reorganized in May and November 1992 to ensure that relatives of missing persons would have an input in the work of the Committee. Changes were also made in May 1993 to reflect the interests of the newly-elected Kuwaiti Parliament.

3 See in particular UN Security Council resolutions 686 (1991) and 687 (1991).

4 These included stateless residents of Kuwait *(bidoun)* who had not been employed by the Government of Kuwait; Jordanian citizens, including those of Palestinian origin; and other Palestinians.

5 On this list were 1,583 Kuwaiti citizens, 354 stateless residents of Kuwait (bidoun), 2 nationals of the United Arab Emirates, 60 Saudis, 16 Syrians, 29 Egyptians, 1 Omani, 13 Lebanese, 1 Somali, 3 Bahrainis, 7 Filipinos, 13 Indians, 4 Pakistanis, 14 Iranians and 1 Sri Lankan.

6 Established at the third round of ICRC-Sponsored Riyadh talks between coalition and Iraqi representatives.

7 The initial total of files was 627 but on-going research led to the deletion of several names because their remains were found in Kuwait.

8 Paragraph 2(c).

9 Para.3(c).Resolution 686 also recognised "that during the period required for Iraq to comply with paragraphs 2 and 3 above, [part of which have been quoted] the provisions of paragraph 2 of resolution 678 (1990) remain valid". This latter paragraph is the one which authorized Member States of the United Nations cooperating with the Government of Kuwait, "to use all necessary means to uphold and implement Security Council resolution 660 (1990) and all subsequent relevant resolutions and to restore international peace and security in the area".

10 Paragraph 31 also invited "the International Committee of the Red Cross to keep the Secretary-General apprised as appropriate of all activities undertaken in connection with facilitating the repatriation or return of all Kuwaiti and third country nationals or their remains present in Iraq on or after 2 August 1990".

11 Para 21.

12 The search for missing persons and the release and repatriation of Kuwaiti and third country detainees is, however, only one aspect of the issue of compliance. Iraq's commitment to eliminate weapons of mass destruction is of more immediate concern to members of the Security Council. Other Iraqi commitments included the return of Kuwaiti property stolen during the occupation and the demarcation of boundaries between Iraq and Kuwait.

13 The Security Council also requested the Secretary-General in consultation with the International Committee of the Red Cross "submit within 20 days of the date of adoption of this resolution a report to the Security Council on activities undertaken in accordance with paragraph 31 of resolution 687 (1991) in connection with facilitating the repatriation or return of all Kuwaiti and third country nationals or their remains present in Iraq on or after 2 August 1990".

14 UN doc. E/CN.4/1992/64.

15 The lists also refer to 83 people whose repatriation to Kuwait had been rejected by the Kuwaiti authorities; 146 foreigners and Arabs who had been handed over through the mission of the ICRC; 12 dead also handed over through the mission of the ICRC; 2,007 "people registered through their embassies" and, finally, 21 Al-Sabah family members who were repatriated to Kuwait in April 1991.

16 See *Report on the situation of human rights in Kuwait under Iraqi occupation,* prepared by Mr. Walter Kälin, Special Rapporteur of the Commission on Human Rights, in accordance with Commission resolution 1991/67, p41.

17 S/23472.

18 Dated 16 January 1992.

19 More than 20 convoys of persons who were living freely in Iraq have returned to Kuwait under the auspices of the ICRC since spring 1991. Kuwait had to be particularly careful in processing applications for repatriation since Iraq had already used a certain flexibility in visa applications to infiltrate more than 400 commandos into Kuwait in June 1990.

20 See section on the ICRC.

21 See Report of 25 January 1992 of the Secretary-General on the status of compliance by Iraq with the obligations placed upon it under certain of the Security Council resolutions relating to the situation between Iraq and Kuwait. S/23514.

22 Letter to the Secretary-General dated 6 March 1992 by the representatives of Kuwait, Saudi Arabia, United Kingdom and United States in response to Iraq's letter of 28 February.

23 ibid.

24 UN Commission on Human Rights, Resolution 1991/67, The Situation of Human Rights under Iraqi Occupation, 4 June 1991.

25 E/CN.4/1992/26,: Report on the situation of human rights in Kuwait under Iraqi occupation, prepared by Mr Walter Kälin, Special Rapporteur of the Commission on Human

Rights, in accordance with Commission resolution 1991/67.
26 E/CN.4/1992/84, at 140. UN Commission on Human Rights, Resolution 1992/60 The Situation of Human Rights in Kuwait under Iraqi Occupation.
27 UN Commission on Human Rights, Resolution 1992/71, E/CN.4/1992/84. at 166-8.
28 Including:
"(a)Summary and arbitrary executions, orchestrated mass executions and burials, extrajudicial killings, including killings, in particular in the northern region of Iraq, in southern Shiah centres and in the southern marshes;
(b) Widespread routine practice of systematic torture in its most cruel forms, including the torture of children;
(c) Enforced or involuntary disappearances, routinely practised arbitrary arrest and detention, including of women and children, consistent and routine failure to respect due process and the rule of law;
(d) hostage-taking and the use of persons as "human shields" a most grave and blatant violation of Iraq's obligations under international law".
29 Resolution 47/145, Situation of Human Rights in Iraq, 18 December 1992.
30 U.N. doc. S/25012.
31 Quoted as follows:
"The first list contained 11,431 names and was submitted in April 1991
The second list contained 5,433 names and was submitted in May 1991
The third list contained 4,290 names and was submitted in June 1991
The fourth list contained 2,479 names and was submitted in September 1991
The fifth list contained 2,443 names and was submitted in October 1991
The sixth list contained 2,201 names and was submitted in March 1992
The seventh list contained 850 names and was submitted in March 1992."
32 In a letter to the Secretary-General of the Security Council, UN doc. S/25758, and in a letter dated 10 June from the Permanent Representative of Iraq to the United Nations, addressed to the Secretary General, UN doc. S/25928.
33 In a letter dated 17th May 1993, addressed to the President of the Security Council.
34 UN doc. S/25790; see also letter to the President of the Security Council, July 1993, UN doc. S/26103
35 Iraq permitted the Secretary-General's special emissary to visit Baghdad in January 1994.
36 UN doc. S/26449.
37 Amnesty International: *Iraq, secret detention of Kuwaitis and third country nationals.* AI Index: MDE 14/05/93
38 Diplomatic note dated 11 November 1991 from the Permanent Mission of Iraq, addressed to the ICRC.
39 The ICRC have had limited access to Abu Ghraib, jail outside of Baghdad in which foreigners detained by the Iraqi Government are generally housed, including those who inadvertently crossed into Iraq from Kuwait and were incarcerated in Abu Ghraib. A Kuwaiti national was reported missing in May 1993 and discovered in Abu Ghraib in January 1994 where he was serving an eight-year prison term for illegal entry.

LEGAL BACKGROUND
1 Article 96(2) of Additional Protocol I.
2 On 8 August 1990 Iraq dismissed the transitional Government it had placed in power in Kuwait and proclaimed the annexation of Kuwait. On 28 August, it was announced that the area of Kuwait bordering Iraq had been incorporated as an extension of the province of Basra. The rest of Kuwait was declared to be the nineteenth province of Iraq.
3 SC Resolution 662(1990), 9 August 1990 and SC Resolution 664(1990), 18 August 1990. Both resolutions declared that the annexation of Kuwait by Iraq under any form and whatever pretext had no legal validity, and was to be considered null and void.
4 Article 42 of the Hague Regulations states that "[t]erritory is considered occupied when it is actually placed under the authority of the hostile army. The occupation extends only to territory where such authority has been established and can be exercised".
5 Article 43 of the Hague Regulations. The full text reads as follows:
"The authority of the legitimate power having in fact passed into the hands of the occupant, the latter shall take all measures in his power to restore, and ensure, as far as possible, public order and safety, while respecting, unless absolutely prevented, the laws in force in the country". See also Articles 64 and 65 of the fourth Geneva Convention.
6 According to Article 4 of the Covenant, States may take measures derogating from their obligations under the Covenant "[i]n time of public emergency which threatens the life of

the nation" but only "to the extent strictly required by the exigencies of the situation". The rights contained in Articles 6,7,8 (paragraphs 1 and 2),11,15,16 and 18 are non-derogable, which means that they apply unconditionally even in time of emergency.

[7] Even though Article 2, paragraph 1 of the International Covenant binds each State party "to respect and to ensure to all individuals within its territory and subject to its jurisdiction" the rights contained in the Covenant, this has been authoritatively interpreted as not barring the extraterritorial application of the Covenant when the alleged violations take place on foreign territory, provided that the perpetrator of the violation acting on foreign soil is an agent of a State party to the Covenant. See discussion to this effect in the *Report on the situation of human rights in Kuwait under Iraqi occupation*, prepared by Walter Kälin, Special Rapporteur of the Commission on Human Rights. E/CN.4/1992/26, 16 January 1992.

[8] Article 2 common to all four Geneva Conventions states that all four conventions apply "to all cases of declared war or of any other armed conflict which may arise between two or more of the High Contracting Parties, even if the state of war is not recognized by one of them" and that "[t]he Conventions shall also apply to "all cases of partial or total occupation of the territory of a High Contracting Party even if the said occupation meets with no armed resistance". The Security Council categorically rejected Iraq's assertion that it was not an occupying force because it considered Kuwait to be Iraqi territory. The Security Council also affirmed in resolution 674 (1990) of 29 October 1990 "that the fourth Geneva Convention applied to Kuwait and that as a High Contracting Party to the Convention, Iraq was bound to comply fully with its terms.

[9] It should be noted that under the third Geneva Convention the category of persons entitled to POW status is more extensive than that favoured with the right to bear arms. For instance authorized civilians accompanying the armed forces, including supply contractors, accredited war correspondents, as well as civilian members of air or sea crews are entitled to POW status on capture but they are not entitled to fight.

[10] Contained in Article 4 (A)(2) of the third Geneva Convention. Militia and volunteer corps who do not form part of the regular army must also comply with these conditions.

[11] Belonging to a party to the conflict may mean that the resistance movement are associated with a Government in exile. In the case of the Kuwaiti resistance, this would have been the Kuwaiti Government in exile in Taif with which they seem to have had close ties.

[12] Article 44(1).

[13] Article 44(3).

[14] A number of these seem to have been reservists or retired or demobilised military personnel whose identity papers may have linked them to the security forces. Article 4 (B)(1) of the third Convention allows for the granting of POW status and the internment of "[p]ersons belonging, or having belonged, to the armed forces of the occupied country, if the occupying Power considers it necessary by reason of such allegiance to intern them..."

[15] Article 21 of the third Geneva Convention .

[16] If any doubt arises as to the determination of POW status, combatants must be treated as prisoners of war until the matter has been decided by a competent tribunal (Article 5).

[17] Article 12.

[18] Article 13.

[19] Article 10 of the third Convention provides that in the event of Protecting Powers (independent States appointed by the parties to the conflict to look after the interests of their nationals) or other organizations agreed by the parties to the conflict not being appointed, "the Detaining Power shall request, or shall accept, subject to the provisions of this Article, the offer of the services of a humanitarian organization, such as the International Committee of the Red Cross, to assume the humanitarian functions performed by Protecting Powers under the present Convention". See also Article 126 which states that "Representatives or delegates of the Protecting Powers shall have permission to go to all places where prisoners of war may be, particularly to places of internment, imprisonment and labour, and shall have access to all premises occupied by prisoners of war".

[20] Article 7.

[21] Amnesty International does not make any distinction in the current status of civilians and military personnel who remain unaccounted for in Iraq, but considers their continued imprisonment, regardless of original reasons for arrest, to constitute arbitrary detention. The organization considers those detainees to be prisoners of conscience who are now held solely on account of their ethnic origin or for their real or perceived association with States which Iraq's Government considers to be its enemies.

[22] Note that prisoners of war may not in general be kept in penitentiaries (Article 22).

[23] Article 120.